Book Publishing 101

▶ **Workbook**

Second Edition

Diane,
I hope this book
gives you many
ideas for your
project.

Freelance Communications

www.bookpublishing101.net

Book Publishing 101 Workbook – Second Edition

Copyright © 2010 Debbie Elicksen

ISBN 978-0-9865956-1-5

Library and Archives Canada Cataloguing in Print

Elicksen, Debbie
Book Publishing 101 Workbook – Second Edition/Debbie Elicksen

1. Publishers and publishing – Handbooks, manuals, etc.
2. Book industries and trade – Handbooks, manuals, etc.
3. Self-publishing – Handbooks, manuals, etc.
4. Authorship – Handbooks, manuals, etc. I. Title.

Z283.E45 2010 070.5 C2010-902482-6

Printed in the United States of America

Publisher
Booklocker.com, Inc.

About Self-Publishing 101 (the First Book)

"Mission accomplished. The response to our book has been TREMENDOUS. Your book helped enormously. Thank you."
Evelyn C. White, Author, Every Goodbye Ain't Gone: A Photo Narrative of Black Heritage on Salt Spring Island www.dancingcrowpress.com

"Your book 'Self-Publishing 101' was instrumental in the success of my book. I read and re-read your work and followed it step by step. Your book was easy to follow and your explanations were clear and understandable as I journeyed through the publishing process. All topics were helpful, however the templates/examples of the business/marketing plans and release/consent forms were for me the most useful.

"Thanks to your advice, I crafted the process for a book cover 'that jumps off the shelf.' I pursued the vanity publishing option and contacted a consultant to help me with the design and layout process. Unknown to me, the consultant had his own publishing company (Chesapeake Books Company, Baltimore, Maryland) and after receiving and reading my draft, he requested that his company publish the book. During all publishing negotiations, processes, printing and in addressing various issues that seemed to pop up at every turn, your book proved valuable for resource and reference information and in the establishing of marketing benchmarks. I do not believe my work would have been a success if not for your book and I just wanted to thank you."
Joseph B. Ross Jr., Author, Arundal Burning
http://arundelburning.com/

"Debbie Elicksen's book Self-Publishing 101 was an amazing resource that we used in navigating the exciting and successful journey of bringing the dream of this book to reality. It takes a lot of work, but is well worth the effort when you experience the joy of knowing your book is impacting its readers."
Annette Stanwick, Forgiveness: The Mystery and Miracle
www.annettestanwick.com

"The book provides solid content, organization to die for, a brutally honest approach, a fast-paced style, and lots of helpful extras. It provides both encouragement and a healthy measure of reality to a writer considering publishing a manuscript."
Janet Arnett, Canadian Book Review Annual, March/April 2007

"I recommended your book to a group of writers attending my "Insiders Guide to Getting Published" workshop I held here at Humber. And it's on the recommended reading list for my program."
Cynthia Good, Program Director, The Creative Book Publishing Program, School for Creative and Performing Arts

Table of Contents

10 Steps to Book Publishing

Introduction

Everyone wants to write the Great North American Novel. For most who try, just getting started is difficult and the process can be very overwhelming. And when they do get it started, they soon discover obtaining a traditional publisher is harder than getting an audience with the Pope.

There are things a potential author needs to know before they solicit a royalty publisher or decide to do it themselves. Having gone through the publishing process several times over and by soliciting expertise from others even more experienced than me, this workbook will provide you with the necessary steps to help you sift through the maze of uncertainty and give you the courage to follow your dream of producing an actual book.

My purpose for doing this:

a. Dispel the myths of publishing
b. Inspire would-be authors with the courage to go forward
c. Improve the professionalism of a self-published book so nobody can tell the difference

I've been providing full publishing support to independent and self-publishers who want to get their message across in books for several years, and through this process, I've come up with three things every would-be author needs to know:

1. By understanding the publishing process and what's involved, the author can see and believe in the fact that they, too, can publish a book.
2. Regardless if they self-publish or land a traditional publisher, they need to do the due diligence in creating a professional product that would be welcome in any bookstore.
3. No matter what the venue or how the book is published, the author has to come up with a succinct and ongoing marketing plan.

There are so many options for authors to get published today, including traditional publishers, small publishers, self-publishing, and print-on-demand publishing. It's no wonder that inexperienced authors have a tough time finding the right option for their books. This workbook will arm authors with the information they need to make the right choices.

This workbook acts as an addendum to the bestselling Self-Publishing 101 (Self-Counsel Press), but it can also be used on its own. Much of the information has been updated from the Self-Publishing 101 book and more has been added to the previous edition of the Book Publishing 101 Workbook.

Step 1

Everyone Has a Book in Them

Where do you begin?

Whether you are a seasoned writer or a novice – a lot of people have trouble trying to figure out where to start on their manuscript. Even if you have 70 books under your belt, the most intimidating image is a blank white Microsoft Word page. You squirm in your chair, get up and pet the cat, go phone a friend, watch TV, and basically do everything to avoid that big blank page.

It took Michelangelo from 1508 to 1512 to paint the Sistine Chapel. It isn't really uncommon for a manuscript to take that long, either. It depends on where you are at in your life.

The blank page

If you haven't begun yet and it's been in the back of your mind for a while now; if you've started it and haven't gotten around to finishing; if you're just one chapter away – forget about it. Don't beat yourself up. When you are ready, wild horses will not stop you. That manuscript will take on a life of its own once your mind and body are so ready, you can't think of doing anything else until you finish it. But sometimes, a little thing, a thought, a TV show, a picture will spur that thought and off you go.

In the meantime, these are exercises to get your thought molecules working.

Vera Goodman (www.readingwings.com) is gifted at getting people writing – particularly children and families writing together. She offers exercises that provide a unique angle twist. Instead of describing a scene or character as a narrator or from that character's perspective – describe the scene or character from a totally different viewpoint. For example:

- Describe a hockey player's shift on the ice from his stick's perspective or the puck's perspective.

- Describe Paris Hilton from her purse's point of view.

- Describe an accountant's meeting with a client from his pencil's point of view.

English author Richard Adams has skillfully penned several novels in this way. He wrote the classic tale "Watership Down," about of a group of rabbits living in their own environment and their interaction with humans from the rabbits' point of view. His book "Plague Dogs" was about two mistreated dogs that had escaped a government research facility from the dogs' viewpoint.

See the picture below?

Write one paragraph about what you see in this picture. How is it speaking to you? Who is this girl? What are her thoughts? What's her story? There is no right or wrong way to do this. You can write it prose, poetry, point form – however you like. Just tell her story in one paragraph.

Paragraph

When it comes to developing the manuscript, sometimes a picture like this will compel you to write a fictional story. The paragraph you wrote could be fleshed out into several chapters. It could be the start of your manuscript.

How to find other ideas to write about

Other examples of trying to come up with something to write start with looking at yourself, your environment, and your passions.

- What do you do that you or other people think is special?

- What advice do people come to you for over and over again, whether it's your kids, your neighbors, work associates. Sometimes they perceive you as the expert in some area. It could be parenting, gardening, anything. It could be your work.

- What are some things that have happened to you that you can help inspire others? A lot of people might write about challenges, whether it's cancer or some other disease. If you were to develop diabetes overnight, would you want to read a book by someone who was going through the same thing? Would you want to learn some tips on how they coped with it? Think about other types of experiences or it could be about dumb things kids do, pet tricks.

- What's your expertise in your work? Are you a banker, accountant, electrician? If you've been doing it for a while, you've developed some skills and industry insight. Maybe a textbook on engineering might not be a compelling read but you could find different angles to tweak that. How do you get into the engineering business? How different would it be now to get into it?

- Sometimes your dreams might create the next great plot, but only if you write them down as soon as you wake up. Your environment, what you watch on television, and what you read can culminate into some strange and compelling storylines.

You can write. Seriously. It doesn't matter who you are and how much writing or reading you've done – you CAN write, especially when you apply some of the simple editing tools from Step 4.

But the one thing you need to also keep in mind when you are developing a writing angle is: why would someone read your story?

It isn't really about you; it's about the reader. You might think about coming up with something that would make them want to read it.

You could do a manuscript on the history of your family. You're not necessarily going to sell that on Oprah's book club. But your purpose might be to share your story and your family's history with future generations. What a great gift to keep the story ongoing. Remember the mini-series "Roots," where Kunta Kinte is captured from Gambia as a slave and throughout his tormented journey, he passes down the family stories of his grandmother about an African ancestor.

Find a purpose behind your writing. You might want to help people through a challenge, using your own story to back it up.

You can find a way to promote your business through writing a book by offering solid expertise.

Other questions that might tweak your storyline:

- What do you have to offer the world?

- What experiences can you share that might help or encourage others?

- What is your expertise?

- Why would someone be interested in your story?

- What ways can you promote your business through books?

- What do you do that is different from everyone else?

- What advice do you get asked for all the time?

- What are you most known for?

- Why are customers buying your service?

- What are your business strengths and weaknesses?

- What is the trend in your industry?

- How have you identified your customers' needs?

- How has the industry changed since you started?

- What are some of the challenges you faced while growing your business?

- How do your management skills impact your staff?

- Explain your role in the industry.

- Why do people find you fascinating?

- What do you say to those just starting out?

- What isn't being said in your industry?

A lot of times, just getting started is half the battle. Hopefully those questions will help get you thinking about what you have going on in your own life that you can write about.

Conquering the fear of writing

What's the worst that can happen?

> Find a reason to write
> Face a challenge and do it anyway
> Take a risk, grow, and learn from your mistakes

You can take steps to conquer the fear by rewriting a magazine, blog, or newspaper article or writing it from a different angle.

You can write a comparison between a book and a movie, looking at how they differ and what is similar. Some examples of books that were made into movies are The Godfather, The Shining, North and South, Of Mice and Men.

When I was a kid, I used to make up play-by-plays of games that never happened, such as The Stanley Cup That Wasn't – between the Boston Bruins and the Chicago Blackhawks. I used to also transcribe the play-by-play of junior hockey games.

Every picture has a story, such as the exercise on page 9.

Find a song you like, Google the lyrics, and write your own words. Morning radio programs seem to do this all the time.

Another thing some radio stations do is create their own versions of plays. I remember years ago, when Humble Howard and the morning crew on a popular radio station in Calgary did their own remake of the Wizard of Oz. It was quite funny. Will always remember "and Doug Gossen Garland as Dorothy."

You can always rewrite the ending to one of your favorite books.

Getting used to writing

I'm sorry to have to tell you this, but the only way you can become a great writer is to write. Practice writing – it's the only way to get better at it.

Journal. It's a way to get stuff on paper. When you're journaling, you don't have to worry about editing. You're just throwing the words on the page. That's where writing starts.

Blogging is another way to publish your stories and get you serious about writing, because they'll be in the public domain.

There is no right or wrong way to pen a manuscript

If you look at all the books in the bookstores and on your shelves at home, you're going to see every different kind of format and style. Some are letters and diaries, like Bram Stoker's Dracula. There are picture books. The variety is endless. What's right for you is whatever inspires you. It's about your own personal vision as to how you see the end result.

There's no sense in reinventing the wheel. You can take ideas from the books that are on your shelves. They can help you figure out how to develop the manuscript.

Start with that scary blank white page. It's quite intimidating. But once you throw some words on it, they just keep falling out. Once you get that first sentence on there, it just keeps going. But it's getting that first sentence that is really hard. It doesn't matter who you are. You can be a professional writer in business for 50 years. You still have the same anxiety when it comes to the blank page.

Another way to figure out what to write is to ask yourself what you are most passionate about. If you could erase whatever you're doing right now and go into your dream job today, what would that be? It might not be a job. You could be passionate about squirrels. You know everything about them, collect everything that has anything to do with them, and watch them frequently.

Not in sequence

When you're throwing the words on the paper (Microsoft Word file), keep in mind that, like movies, books aren't necessarily written in sequence. You can just have some topic ideas. Those topic ideas will eventually shape into chapters. At the beginning, it's just throwing stuff into the box in the corner. Throw it on the page as it comes to your brain. Throw it in a file folder. Use whatever works easiest for you as an organizing tool.

When it comes time to write anything for your manuscript, just throw the words down. Save the editing for later. If you edit while you write, 20 years from now, you will still be in the same place you are now.

Tools

Pocket tape recorder

You can use a pocket tape recorder to take your notes for you. If you teach, if you do any workshops or keynotes, tape yourself and then transcribe it, shape it, and there's a book.

You could carry the tape recorder around with you to catch an idea as it comes to you. That's usually easier to do than writing while you're driving on a freeway. Because once the seed is planted, you're always thinking. You're always developing ideas. The more you write, the more ideas develop, the more they come at the most inopportune moments. Three in the morning is a popular time, so also have a **notebook and a pen** in your nightstand.

When those ideas come, you have to write them down immediately. You will forget them maybe 10 seconds later. It could be the title. It could the first sentence on that blank page. It could be a chapter title. It could be your best marketing plan.

Transcribing software programs

Dragon Naturally Speaking is probably the best program out there. Although you do have to take some time to train any of those programs to know your voice. They will still invent words but it's kind of fun to watch it transcribe as you speak.

Interns/"volunteers"

You might have someone up your sleeve who can transcribe tape for you or help you with some of the research.

My mentor in New York has a host of interns who have helped him with his 100-plus books. The interns are usually journalism students who want to learn more about the publishing/media industry. You might be able to find a high school student who could use the experience towards his/her credits.

Defining the work

What's your favorite book? What are some other books that you really like the layout of? Are they fiction or non-fiction?

- Alice Cooper's book talks about how he transferred his addiction from alcohol to golf. It's laid out in regular chapters. There are no subtitles in the chapters. (Alice Cooper, Golf Monster by Alice Cooper With Keith and Kent Zimmerman. Three Rivers Press, New York, 2007.)
- Eat, Pray, Love has chapters numbered only. (Eat, Pray, Love by Elizabeth Gilbert. Penguin Books, 2006.)
- Bram Stoker's Dracula has its story told by letters. (Dracula by Bram Stoker. Doubleday, New York, 1897)

In choosing a format, you decide what's easiest for you. It's purely personal. A lot of times a fiction book tends to be similar to another, but why not be different?

Don't worry about editing to start, just get it down on "paper."

Think about being a reader. We know that when we pick up some books, we immediately say, "Ugh." How am I going to read this? Sometimes the format turns you off the book. It's 1,200 pages and each chapter is 150 pages. What's an easy read for you? How are the words presented visually? Are they small simple chapters? Are there a lot of subheadings? If you find what you like, maybe you can translate that same format to your book.

You could write it in first, second, or third person. You can do it in a diary format, letters, or memos.

First person is when a character is observing the story first-hand. The narrator uses "I" or "we." The following is an example from Edgar Allan Poe's classic tale "The Tell-tale Heart" (Complete Stories and Poems of Edgar Allan Poe. Doubleday, New York, 1966).

> It was open – wide, wide open – and I grew furious as I gazed upon it. I saw it with perfect distinctness – all a dull blue, with a hideous veil over it that chilled the very marrow in my bones; but I could see nothing else of the old man's face or person: for I had directed the ray as if by instinct, precisely upon the damned spot.

Second person tells the story to another character: "you." This is from "The Secret" by Rhonda Byrne (Beyond Words Publishing, Oregon and Atria Books, New York, 2006).

> The only reason why people do not have what they want is because they are thinking more about what they *don't* want than what they *do* want. Listen to your thoughts, and listen to the words you are saying. The law is absolute and there are no mistakes.

In third person, the narrator sees all the action in the story and tells it from a "he/she" perspective. This example is from Leon Uris's "Mila 18" (Bantam Books, New York, Toronto 1961).

> "It's swarming with Germans. They must be looking for our bunker."

> Wolf and Simon felt Chris writhe as spears of pain lashed up and down his leg. Chris's leg twitched against Wolf's face. Simon handed Chris a handkerchief. "Bite on this," he said.

> Luminous eyes peered at the four strangers who had invaded their home. A scraping of claws.

> "Rats!"

You have an idea what you want to write about. Say the book is non-fiction about romance. Some of the topics might be:

- Romance after divorce
- What to do on a first date
- Who pays
- Traditional and non-traditional
- Internet
- Dating when you have kids
- Romance on a budget
- Dating in the workplace
- Dating someone from another culture

Sometimes, we'll come up with the topics before we figure out where the book is going. When you look at the topics on the previous page, you can write a book on romance and the topics are the chapter heads. Some of them might only be subheadings because they're not meaty enough to stand on their own. They could be individual book topics, too.

Breaking it down into topics

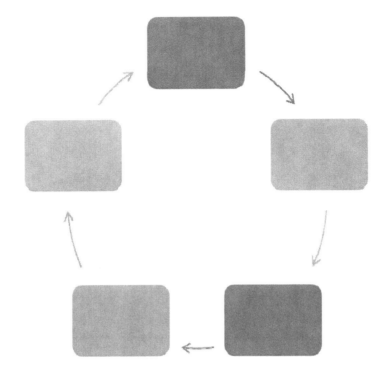

Organize your topics

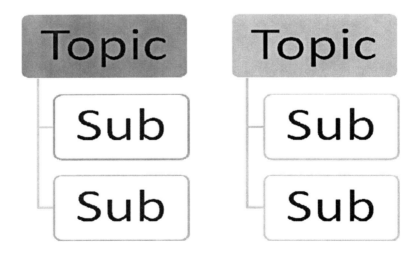

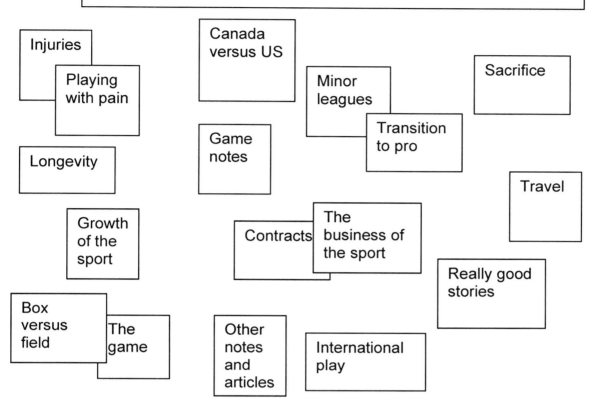

Loose notes and interviews broken into various topics for *Loyalty, Intensity, and Passion: A behind the scenes look at the National Lacrosse League* (ISBN 978-0-9730237-5-6)

Injuries

Playing with pain

Canada versus US

Minor leagues

Sacrifice

Transition to pro

Longevity

Game notes

Travel

Growth of the sport

Contracts

The business of the sport

Really good stories

Box versus field

The game

Other notes and articles

International play

Do all the topics stand alone? Or are there some that might be subtopics?

When you list topic ideas, you're basically itemizing your chapters or subheadings.

If you were the resident expert on romance, you could start your book out as a general book on the topic, then you can get more specific in honing in on specific areas for the next book.

Your book idea:

List topics that might go into the book:

Organize topics

In fiction writing, one needs to consider plots and settings, besides the characters.

If you write fiction, and going back to the paragraph you wrote about the girl with the cat on page 8, if you were going to flush that out…say the girl's name was Ellen…

Who are the other characters in the story?

How do they get introduced?

What do they do?

What are their physical characteristics?

Besides hair color and body image, you need to know your characters' passions, their emotional state, how they react to stress. Because if you don't introduce Ellen again until five chapters later, you can go back and remind yourself about her and how she fits into the story. The more you know about the character, the more you can develop the story around them.

You almost need to have a workbook beside you to keep track of each character, setting, and event. Why? You will never remember every word you write, contrary to what might be popular belief.

When someone is developing fiction, that person tends to look at the people in his or her own life for characteristics. You don't have to use their names. Some people have storylines they can use by inserting different characters and details.

Donelle	35	Black male, glasses, mover and shaker, ladies' man, likes sports, plays basketball and lacrosse, hates being cold, 6'2"…	Bank lender	Main character
Clarissa	26	Blonde female, likes tennis and badminton, somewhat insecure, 5'7"…	Retail clerk at JC Penny	Girlfriend
Drew	18	Red-headed white male, just graduated from high school…	Not working	Donelle and Clarissa meet him in Chapter Five when he…

Use other books to see how they introduce characters. Dialogue is important. Some books are just dialogue. You're telling the story through people talking. But you also have to be cognizant of tense and first, second, or third person and make sure it is consistent.

What works for one person doesn't necessarily work for another. There are numerous ways to develop a manuscript or keep track of the topics or characters. Find what works best for you.

The title

Sometimes the hardest thing to write in a book is the title. You also can't apply for ISBNs or go too far forward on the book's production until you have a title. So if you're having trouble on the title, you're not alone. It's a hard thing to write, even though it seems very simple.

There are several ideas on how to figure out a title. If you go through magazines and newspapers, look at the advertising and the article headings.

Perhaps the best title for your book might be somewhat self-descriptive. That would help people figure out what the book is about before they pull it off the shelf.

There is no copyright on a title, but you probably don't want to use somebody else's. You might find a similar phrase in a title or a different version, but try to find something that will stick you apart from anybody else. If you go on Amazon/Borders and Chapters/Indigo to see what is out there in the genre you want to write about, that will give you ideas. You also want to check titles so you don't use someone else's accidentally verbatim.

It is almost easier to write the manuscript than the title in some respects. This small piece of prose is used to draw the reader into the book.

Research

Fiction or non-fiction, the quality of your research could make or break your book. If you look at fiction authors Leon Uris and James Michener, their books are heavily researched. They take fictional characters and place them into real historical settings. The historical aspect is very much true.

The Internet

Google is your best friend. Just be mindful that some information out there is opinion rather than fact. You have to decide if the research is real or not. Just look at the 2008 American presidential election to see how untruths can be perceived as truths. Do as much as you can to back up the facts.

Going back to the romance topic, if you go to the Internet, use bookseller sites like Chapters/Indigo, Amazon/Borders, and put in as a search word "romance," or better, fine-tuning that to something more specific, such as "romance and culture." If there are over 50 books that come up on that topic, what you want to do is go in and find a way to adjust the angle so it stands apart from the rest. But it will also list books that you might want to read to add to your research.

Interviews

Another part of research is interviewing people. Getting back to the romance topic, you could talk to romance experts. Maybe there is a doctor you could interview to about the physical aspects of romance, such as the endorphins that are released when we are in love.

My first book Inside the NHL Dream is filled with quotes from National Hockey League personnel. Sometimes you will not get who you want to interview so you must have a plan B. As accredited media, for this book, I approached the players themselves, showed them the outline and cover then asked them questions. For the couple of players I really wanted, I emailed their club's PR directors to arrange to meet with them when they arrived in town. (The success of that task depended on how well the PR director responded, otherwise you just took your chances in the locker room.)

Some of the questions I asked were:

- How difficult of an adjustment was it from junior hockey to the NHL?
- (To Grant Fuhr) Describe what made the Oilers dream team so special?
- (To seasoned veterans) How has the game changed since you began playing?
- (To player agents) What kind of things do you look for in a player?
- Do you ever consider your work hard work?
- How do you handle the pressures?
- If you were Commissioner Gary Bettman, what would you do to improve the league?

Developing your own personal cheat sheet

Who is your favorite broadcaster or interviewer on television or radio? Who gets all the big interviews? Mine are Bill Kurtis, Tom Brokaw, and Barbara Walters. Whenever I watch Barbara Walters, I have a pen and paper handy to jot down the questions she asks, then I rework them to fit to who I'm interviewing.

If I were writing about the trucking industry, I'd want to talk to the Truckers Association president or spokesperson, people from various trucking companies – those who transport energy, perishable foods, or grain – to see what's involved in each industry. I'd also inquire about logistics. How do they move supplies in and out of the warehouse? Does a computer do this?

For example, I interviewed the logistics company for Wal-Mart's one million square foot warehouse in Calgary that services all 50 plus stores in Western Canada. There were 50 plus bays, so when a truck arrived to drop off product, the items (marked by store barcode) travelled via conveyor belt to the other side of the warehouse and onto a waiting truck to take them to that store. The whole process took something like 15 minutes for an item to move from one bay to the other.

I've used email for a lot of interview requests but it's important to proof (and not just by spell check) and not have it look like spam. Regular mail is slow for setting up interviews.

Use the Internet as a research tool to find or learn more about your potential interviews. Plug in key words and started filtering through the sites, saving some in "favorites" so you can access them later. If you want to talk to someone local, just pick up the phone. Not everyone will be accepting of an interview.

Sometimes, as you start interviewing people, ideas will evolve and your book may expand or turn into something a bit different than you initially intended.

When you get to a certain point in the research, the book starts writing itself. It starts telling you what to do.

Once you have a lot of the research and all those topics together, you can start figuring out where you want this thing to go. Some of the interviews might make you go back to those topics and take out a few because they no longer fit. And you might also add more based on something that came up during the interview.

If you don't have enough material on one of the topics, throw it out. That's a difficult thing to do. Nobody will know what you left out. Much like if you were preparing a keynote speech and forgot to talk about a point, chances are the audience will have no idea you left something out. They just know the gist of the message. If it doesn't fit, it doesn't fit. You can't make it fit, and if you do, it upsets the flow of the book.

Copyright

First, you need to know what plagiarism is. It's the difference between borrowing and stealing. You can borrow people's ideas and topics. You can quote people; you just need to name where that source came from. It's when you don't name your source and pass the material off as your own when it becomes plagiarism. This also applies to websites. If you cut and paste something from the Internet into your document and pretend it doesn't have any copyright, it does. You can instead paraphrase, put it into your own words. Always credit your source, even if you're not quoting them verbatim.

A good example would be studies. We all like to cite statistics from a study. In always quoting your source, you are also covering yourself. Don't give people a chance to come back and challenge your work.

Ideas are not copyrightable, but when those ideas are put into physical form, they are. Look how many sales books are on the market. The ideas and mechanics of most of those books are pretty similar. They all say close to the same thing but in a different way. It's that different way – how the author puts the words on the paper – that is copyrighted. If 15 people in your neighborhood wrote about the exact same topic, you would have 15 different reports. It's unlikely anyone will come up with the exact same wording as someone else.

Permissions

If you want to use something from another book, you can go to the publisher to ask if you could use the material. You will find the publisher information on the copyright page in the beginning pages of the book – also by searching online. The publisher will want to know everything about where you intend to use the material, the context to which it will be used, and what passages you want to use.

Comics are copyrighted. You can't just use a comic or any other image without the artist/photographer's permission. In many instances, you will be asked to pay for the rights to use it.

There are stock sites for both comics and images. For pictures, try www.gettyimages.com, www.istock.com, www.photos.com, www.masterfile.com, and www.veer.com. For comics, try www.thecomicbank.com and other stock sites you can search for through Google.

If you see a comic you would like to use, you can use the search engine on the stock comic site and input the artist's name to find the image. Sometimes it takes a bit of elbow grease to find the source of the image. Unless it is with a stock site, you might not always get permission. For example, Dilbert and Far Side comics are very particular as to who can use their images. Unless you fit that category, you'll be denied. Other comics might lead you straight to the artist, who will want to know more about your project and how you intend to use the comic.
For photo sites, you can key in a topic in the search engine and the site will give you a series of images that fit that topic.

If you have any questions as to what a permission form might look like, you can Google "permission request" and find some examples.

Table of Contents

You have your topic list, so all you need to do is look at it to see what comes first. There is no scientific way of doing this. You will be reworking it as you go along. But first, it's about organizing your content.

Your topics might not be full chapters. They might be subs. And you might even put your Table of Contents together before you list the topics. It doesn't matter. Whatever is easiest.

If you are going to do a proposal for a publisher, you'll have to take this one step further and describe what each chapter is about – a paragraph description. Sometimes it helps to look at other books to see how those Table of Contents are organized.

The Table of Contents is fluid at the start. Some of it does change. You are going to change your mind about what you put in the book.

Your chapters could flow into each other or stand alone. That's a personal choice. Sometimes it might be the publisher's choice, too.

Once you get to that point of putting the accumulated material into your computer, you start seeing where the manuscript is going to take you. That's where you start making decisions. You see where the gaps are. There might be a topic you don't have very much on, you could throw it out, but you really think it is important to the rest of the book. So you go back and do more research to fill it out.

It's making sense of your notes – organizing them in a way that makes sense for you. You don't have to start chronologically. You can start at the end and go back to the beginning.

You are not alone

At an Independent Publishers Association of Canada meeting in Calgary, someone brought up an issue that every author could relate to: psychological blocks that prevent manuscripts from being finished.

Here are some ways you might address this:

a. Write from a distance: write something and sleep on it before reviewing

b. The block to finish the last pages can mean – now that it's done, what do you do with it? Being a good writer doesn't mean you are a good marketer and visa versa. Find people to play to your weaknesses: hire a marketer or a ghostwriter.

c. The fear factor – being afraid of success or failure – what's the worst that can happen? Manuscripts are highly personal. There can be anxiety about finally releasing it.

d. Projects take a part of your life. It's important. You can't give it up because if you do, there may be nothing to take its place. Maybe start a new manuscript or research another project to fill that void.

Step 2

Your Book's Resume

Simple outline

Once you first put your manuscript together and try to figure out what you're going to do with it, one of the ways you can help yourself is by creating an outline. When you're putting an outline together, it really reaffirms why you wrote the manuscript in first place. This is your book's resume. It helps you describe your manuscript in punchy copywriting terms. It's your elevator speech when somebody asks you: what's your book about?

You need to put these words in very strong simplistic terms so that people get it right off the first sentence.

There are several different ways to do the outline. The outline is also universal for various treatments. It's information about your book that you can give to a potential research interview, to media, to selling your book idea to a publisher, to bookstores, to sponsors, selling it to a distributor, for anyone you want to get the book out to.

The outline is created in an inverted pyramid structure. That means your first paragraph will be the most important part of the whole piece, outside of the title. This paragraph is your elevator speech – your selling tool.

On a one- to two-page outline, the description of your book will be around four to five paragraphs, with the first one being the most important and the last paragraph the least important. In that last paragraph, you will want to include what the reader is going to get out of your book. Why should they read it?

Overall, once a publisher or the media get past the title, they'll read the first sentence. If they get through that, they'll read the first paragraph. That first paragraph will determine the decision – for a publisher if they are going to ask for more information and for the media if they intend to call you for a story. In a lot of cases, even if the outcome is positive, they never read past that first paragraph.

If the title or that first sentence doesn't hold their attention, the outline goes to straight the garbage. You really want it to be crisp, easy, and straight to the point.

But also note that the outline and any other marketing materials related to your book are going to be a work in progress. Nobody ever nails anything right off the bat. We always improve it as we go along.

The outline will eventually turn into a proposal. It encompasses a few paragraphs about what your book is about. It should be some of the best writing that you do, because the clearer you can get on those paragraphs, the better you can sell your book.

The other thing you need to know, and you might want to do some research, particularly if you are trying to enlist the media or a publisher, is you want to know what's on the market. If your book is on sales, for example, and there are a gazillion sales books on the market, you need to know where your sales book fits in with the rest. You need to find out what else is out there that might be similar. If you don't, you can't pretend that other people are not going to know.

If you go for a media interview, they're going to do a little research and ask you what makes your book different than so-and-so's books. If you can't answer that, it doesn't lend you much credibility. You can say, there is this book, this book, and this book out there, but my book says this.

If you already have some interviews done or plan to do some interviews that are significant to what you're writing – impressive interviews, such as the president of the free world or of a major corporation, that might get somebody's attention towards your book. However, you wouldn't write that down unless you intended on getting that interview or already had it. Sometimes an interview will add credibility to your book. But it doesn't have to be an interview. It's the research that goes in behind it. People want to know that you did the due diligence.

Not everybody is going to be interested in reading your book. You want to add to your outline who your target audience is. If it is a book on healthcare, if it is a particular medical topic, think about who would pick up that book; who is your target audience? Figure out who your niche market is and expand it from there. Note that the more you can fine tune who your reader is, the more you can fine tune your marketing.

Next, you'll add the author's qualifications to your outline. What qualifies you to write that book? Why you and not someone else? You may not be working in the industry you are writing about, but it's your passion and you've done a lot of research on it and interviewed a lot of key people. You might have written a book on the mating of parrots, and you have parrots. You've had parrots for 30 years, breeding, raising, and selling them. You know everything there is about parrots. You've studied them, lived with them, and are passionate about them. You put that in the author qualifications because you are the expert in parrots. You have the experience. Or maybe you don't have the experience related to the topic, but you've done the research.

An example of someone that comes to mind is a woman who wrote a book about dealing with hereditary cancer. She interviewed a lot of key people that work in the specific target areas of her topic. Her book has a lot of expertise between her own experience and these interviews. That would qualify her to write it.

Those are the basic elements that make up the outline.

Simple outline

Future Prospects

Future Prospects takes a behind the scenes look into the world of major junior hockey. Focusing on the players' perspective, this book looks at some of the unique aspects of major junior hockey, such as leaving home at a young age, juggling hockey and travel with school commitments, draft issues, and the importance coaches have on their careers and their lives.

Major junior hockey is as close to professional hockey as you can get. Close-knit towns across the country define themselves by their hockey team and take pride in players that graduate to further their careers in the National Hockey League. Even in larger centers like Edmonton and Calgary, in the 1970s, next to professional football, junior hockey was the only game in town.

In *Future Prospects*, players discuss the difficult adjustments they have to make as a player, including the jump from minor hockey to major junior and what it's like to go back to junior after attending a professional hockey camp.

The reader is left with a strong inside knowledge of what it's like to be a player, the challenges faced, the life-long camaraderie, and a few chuckles over some really good stories.

What's on the market:
Lapp, Richard; White, Silas. Local Heroes: A History of the Western Hockey League. Harbour Publishing (ISBN 1550170805), 1993

Lapp, Richard. The Memorial Cup: Canada's National Junior Hockey Championship. Harbour Publishing (ISBN 1550171704), 1997

Various team publications

Target audience: General Canadian audience of all ages, hockey fans

Author's qualifications:
- Authored, edited, ghostwritten, and project managed 100 books
- National Hockey League reporter for over 16 years
- Author and Publisher of *Inside the NHL Dream* (ISBN 09730237-0-8) and *Positive Sports: Professional athletes and mentoring youth* (ISBN 09730237-3-2)
- Author of *Self-Publishing 101*, publisher Self-Counsel Press
- First woman to headman a football team and conference in Canada: Calgary Colts President 1990-1993; Prairie Football Conference President 1996-1998
- Assistant General Manager for eight plus years with the Colts--arranging team travel among other duties, assisting in equipment room for 10 years, issuing equipment, changing facemasks, fitting shoulder pads, packing equipment for road trips and hauling equipment for game day and spring camp
- Long-time major junior hockey supporter

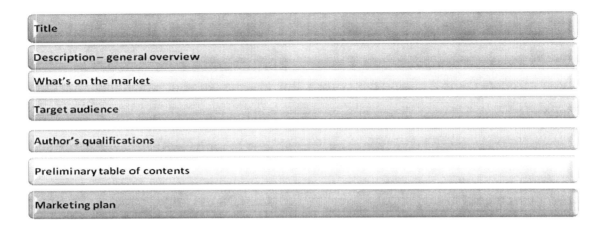

Title

Description– general overview

What's on the market

Target audience

Author's qualifications

Preliminary table of contents

Marketing plan

Outline for publisher

Then there's the outline that you can stretch a little if you are pushing it into a royalty publisher's hands. This would flesh out some of what's already there, for example, with listing the other books on the market, you might use one or two sentences to describe those other books.

You would add in a preliminary table of contents and describe each chapter in some detail that the publisher will understand where you are taking the book.

The extended outline would also include a detailed marketing plan. The better the marketing plan, the more you might interest the publisher.

Sample publisher outline

NHL Entry Draft: dreams made; hearts shattered

Overview

This is a book that will walk the reader through the NHL Entry Draft, showing what it is, how the stage is set, how the players are chosen to enter that stage, and the emotional roller coaster that it can be for each of them. For all of those fortunate to be chosen, it's only the beginning. They still need to do the work to get to training camp and they are a long way off from making a team. For those who aren't chosen or even on the list, it's not always the end of the line. And of those minute few who do get to realize their dream of making that step, this book will act as a guide as to what to expect.

Why do this book? For most sports fans, the great Canadian dream isn't a white house and a picket fence. It's playing in the National Hockey League. When parents sit in the stands at a minor hockey game, sipping their coffee at eight on a Saturday morning, they look towards the ice and think about what it would be like for their son to be the next coming of Sidney Crosby. For any of the players that did make it, yes, they'll tell you it's a wonderful life. But the journey wasn't easy and while getting drafted is a major step, it's only the beginning. Getting to that step is a major feat in itself. Parents, players, and interested fans might like to know the process involved behind the NHL Entry Draft and what it means to get there.

Purpose: A book on the inner workings of the NHL Entry Draft, how it came about, what is involved in putting on the event, and whose lives are affected will document an important part of hockey history. One can go online and garner information about the draft, including some detailed statistics and player profiles, brief blurbs about its history, but even as poignant as some of the profiles might be, there is a myriad of emotions that play into these young lives when they step into this echelon of the arena. It's not always easy to see the real story behind the story.

Knowledge base: I already have numerous documentation and interviews directly related to personal experiences about the NHL Entry Draft. Some of these interviews include NHL and junior league executives, players, agents, and scouts. I have accredited access to the NHL Media site and all NHL and junior games, and anything coming out of Hockey Canada. I receive daily updates and releases from the NHL, Canadian Hockey League, Hockey Canada, and USA Hockey. My hockey library stems back to the 1960s and would rival anything you can find in a public or media library on hockey.

Contribution: Because there are really no books I can find (through Chapters/Indigo, Amazon systems) outside of the NHL draft publications, which I'm not sure are available to the general public, this will be the first book of its kind, so all the information will be new.

Market analysis

Intended audience: Hockey/sports fans of all ages

Uses: I can see this book also being used by player agents to give to their clients to help them prepare for what to expect. A few of those agents already use my *Inside the NHL Dream* book for the same purpose. The Canadian Hockey League is another potential partner to help market the book. They produce an annual guide which accepts outside advertising (it's pretty reasonable) and the deadline is April. Perhaps a partnership arrangement can be made for distribution through each of the CHL centers via their programs or souvenir shops. Through the CHL, there is no concern about NHL licensing issues – only when you do it through the NHL. I can almost guarantee the Western Hockey League and the Alberta Junior Hockey League's cooperation. There are so many minor leagues and development camps that are a natural tie in for the target audience.

Related and competing books: These are the only books I could find that offer brief insight to the NHL Entry draft—

Bylsma, Dan and Jay. So Your Son Wants to Play in the NHL? McClelland and Stewart Inc., Toronto, ISBN 0-7710-1793-6, 1998

Elicksen, Debbie. Inside the NHL Dream. Freelance Communications, Calgary, Alberta, ISBN 09730237-0-8, 2002

Elicksen, Debbie. Positive Sports: Professional athletes and mentoring youth. Freelance Communications, Calgary, Alberta, ISBN 09730237-3-2, 2003

Elicksen, Debbie. Future Prospects. Freelance Communications, Calgary, Alberta, ISBN 09730237-4-0, 2005

Content, structure, and scope

Outline of contents:

1. **In the beginning:** The origins of the draft's history. I would endeavor to include input from those who attended the first draft plus a player or two that were picked, such as Gerry Meehan (the 21st and final pick by Toronto) and Peter Mahovlich (the second pick by Detroit). The NHL initially sponsored amateur teams and changed the system to level the playing field amongst all its teams, giving everyone equal opportunity to acquire players. It was originally called the Amateur Draft and was changed to the Entry Draft in 1979, basically to include those that had played professionally for the defunct World Hockey Association. The issue of draft eligibility has also been an issue over the years. Scotty Munro, who was one of the founders of the Western Hockey League, was incensed by the underage draft.

2. **The big buildup:** There are numerous tournaments for both Junior A and B players leading up to the draft. Many of these events are taken into consideration by Central Scouting, although CS may deny their impact on the rankings. This chapter will focus on the Top Prospects Game, World Junior Championship, and scouting in general. What is the laundry list for teams? What do they look for in a player? What are the logistics about scouting? How does someone get a scouting job?

3. **Central Scouting:** NHL Central Scouting does a detailed evaluation report on each draft-eligible player and provides this information to each NHL club. In 2006, there were nine full-time and six part-time scouts working throughout North America, as well as scouts in Europe (European Scouting). For example, in Jordan Staal's report, it listed him as "a premier forward who is an excellent skater with a wide base style that makes him solid on his skates…" Staal's nickname (Staalzy), his favorite team (Vancouver), favorite player, who had the most influence, and other personal information is included in the report.

4. **Expectations:** Teams have expectations. Sometimes, a player touted for the first pick, even the first round, ends up a bust (1993 – Alexandre Daigle). Sometimes, he more than exceeds expectations (1998 – Vincent Lecavalier). Players have expectations. Some of them believe their own press clippings (1999 – Pavel Brendl). Most sit nervously waiting, surprised they're never picked where Central Scouting ranks them as – it's always several spots or rounds later.

5. **Who goes first? and other media fodder:** There is no doubt draft day is a media event, with live coverage of the first two rounds. Like a US presidential election, the talk and speculation can be almost mind-numbing.

6. **Hoop and holler and a bundle of nerves:** After the players arrive at the draft site, there is a lot going on that builds up to the actual picks. Interviews with teams, press conferences, hotel shuttles, luncheons, and any opportunity to put the players on display. The players just want to get it over with. Everything is all speculation up to now as to where they will go. They just want it over and have a chance to prove they belong.

7. **D-Day – bustle and hustle of everyone who is anyone in hockey:** If the players thought the lead-up was stressful, draft day is a wave of humanity combined with stress, elation, heartbreak, cell phones, microphones, awe, curiosity, interviews, and most of all – boredom. At home, you can turn off the TV. In person, it's excruciating but exciting all at the same time. Everywhere you look, you see the most famous names in hockey.

8. **The silent minority speaks up – scouts have their say:** Draft day is really about the scouts. You see on the draft floor that they hold the cards. Their impressions play a major role as to who gets picked.

9. **Anticipation – the picks:** Players sitting in the stands with their families or waiting by the phone at home – all of them collectively hold their breath as the next name is chosen. This chapter looks at some of those interesting stories of players going through it and the emotions that weigh over them during the process.

10. **Going home and another chance at the draw:** What happens after the draft? What if they're not picked? Players may get two shots at eligibility. There's always next year. If they are picked, chances are they'll hang out with their new team for a while. They'll be treated royally, wined and dined before heading back to the airport.

11. **What's next?** So a player is picked – now what? Does he get invited to training camp? Does he stay in junior or get sent to the minors? Every player has their own anecdote as to the wake-up call that being drafted does not guarantee you a ticket to the big leagues.

Special materials: perhaps a likeness of a hockey card as a bookmark (if there is enough gutter space on the cover printing, can do it at the same time)

Timetable: as soon as there is a go-ahead, it won't take long to gather interviews and material needed to pen the book. I have face-to-face access to a number of teams and players. Many interviews can also be conducted over a coffee or the telephone.

Author's qualifications:

- Authored, edited, ghosted, and project managed over 100 books for both royalty and self-publishers
- National Hockey League and professional sports reporter for over 16 years
- Author and Publisher of
    - *Inside the NHL Dream* (A behind the scenes look at the NHL, ISBN 09730237-0-8)
    - *Positive Sports: Professional athletes and mentoring youth*
    - (ISBN 09730237-3-2)
    - *Future Prospects* (A behind the scenes look at major junior hockey,
    - ISBN 09730237-4-0)
    - *Creating a Legacy: The Calgary Booster Club* (The Calgary Booster Club was the catalyst for bringing Calgary the 1988 Olympic Winter Games, ISBN 09730237-2-4)
    - *Loyalty, Intensity, and Passion* (A behind the scenes look at the National Lacrosse League, ISBN 0-9730237-5-9)
- Author of *Self-Publishing 101*, publisher Self-Counsel Press (2005)
- Appeared on Vicki Gabereau (CTV) and the NHL Network

- City of Calgary Sports Policy Steering Committee
- First woman to headman a football conference in Canada (President of the Prairie Football Conference)
- Public Relations Director for Edmonton Trappers Baseball Club, working closely with the California Angels
- Calgary 1988 Olympic Winter Games, Hockey Committee, Media Liaison
- Canadian Junior Football League, Director of Public Relations and Marketing
- Calgary Colts Junior Football Club, President, Assistant General Manager

Introduction

Imagine you are 18 years old. Against your agent's advice, your parents, who truly believe you are the next coming of Mario Lemieux, insist you fly alone to Columbus for the 2007 National Hockey League Entry Draft so you can accept your team's jersey in person. Preceding scouting reports indicate you'll likely go in the fourth round. Your parents can only afford the one ticket and stay home with your siblings to watch the draft on TV.

After your plane lands in Columbus and you pick up your bags from the baggage turnstile, there is a van waiting for you and a group of other players who arrived from other destinations. With the belongings all loaded and players strapped in, the van then proceeds along International Gateway, steering towards the 670 West/US-62 West/Cassady Avenue exit. Along the 670, the van turns left on Neil Avenue and pulls in front of the media entrance of the Nationwide Arena alongside Nationwide Boulevard. This will be your home for the next few days.

Draft day comes and you're sitting in the lower bowl of the arena – by yourself. There is quite a buzz of activity. About two or three whole sections of the stands are set up as a media area, with tables and plug-ins, where some familiar well-known faces are sprinkled in, talking, working on their laptops, and mulling around.

The floor of the arena has no ice. Instead there are 30 sets of tables with numerous chairs and each table has a sign with its team's name and logo. You can see Brian Burke of the Anaheim Ducks on the phone and several individuals you don't recognize talking all around him. You see Wayne Gretzky from the Phoenix Coyotes, Jacques Lemaire from the Minnesota Wild, Glen Sather of the New York Rangers, and a host of other legends of the game.

There are people sitting intermittently throughout the stands: groups of people representing a player and his family; others who are probably agents assessing the mood of the floor; and interested bystanders who just want to see what the event is all about.

You took a tour of the building and saw the press conference area, where the drafted players have been directed to go after their names are announced, to face the media and questions. There is a podium with a microphone set up in front of a blue backdrop with the NHL logo and the Columbus 2007 Draft logo. The area is basically set up for just the first two rounds.

Your agent checks in on you periodically but he has three other players attending the draft, all touted for the first two rounds and there is an anticipated bidding war for one of them. He does his best to make you feel comfortable and ease your nervousness, but his cell phone is going off every minute. It's almost better without him there.

The first round took the better part of three hours to go through. The second round is almost as long. The whole thing is real long. Because these first two rounds are televised and with there being a set time between picks for teams to make their assessments and put in their order, the day drags. There are a few people you can talk to, mostly rival players in your division. They are at the draft with their families, so it would be uncomfortable for you to sit with them for any length of time. You mostly chat with each other in the concourse.

You sit and wait. Round three rolls by…round four…round five. Your name is still not called. The sixth round comes and goes, and now, your stomach is really starting to clench. Your mouth is dry, regardless of how many bottled waters you drink. Your heart starts pounding. You think about why you're there. Will you get picked? Why does nobody want you? You love your parents but can't help but feel a bit of anger towards them for insisting you be here.

It's the middle of round eight and still no call. You see the hub of tables on the floor area winding down. There are only a few picks left and you can see there are no more deals being made.

The last name is picked and it's not you. You just want to sink into your seat and hide. You don't want anyone to see you and know what a failure you are. You didn't get picked. Out of all those names, yours wasn't one of them. But what about that scouting report? It said you'd go in the fourth. Did everyone lie to you? Your parents? Your agent? Your coach?

This would also include a sample chapter and preface.

Step 3

Treat Your Book Like a New Business

Develop a business plan. Where do you want your book to take you? What's your end goal? If you say money and wealth, nobody cares that you wrote a book. The reader wants to know what's in it for them. Why should he/she invest the time in reading it?

What are you willing to do to maximize its exposure? How do you intend to sell it and get it out to the outside world?

The plan

A business plan is your blueprint for starting any new venture – even a book. A book requires a vision, a dream, and unfortunately, sales. Be as specific as possible in your planning. Use timelines to keep yourself accountable. But if you've never done a business plan, how do you start?

Did you know you have the outline for developing a business plan already in your computer? Depending on how your computer is set up, you can access the PowerPoint template a few ways.

Click on START - then New Office Document (at the top) - then click on the menu Presentations. There is also a template for a marketing plan and project overview that may be helpful.

Open your PowerPoint program directly.

On my Professional XP laptop, here are the pathways I used:

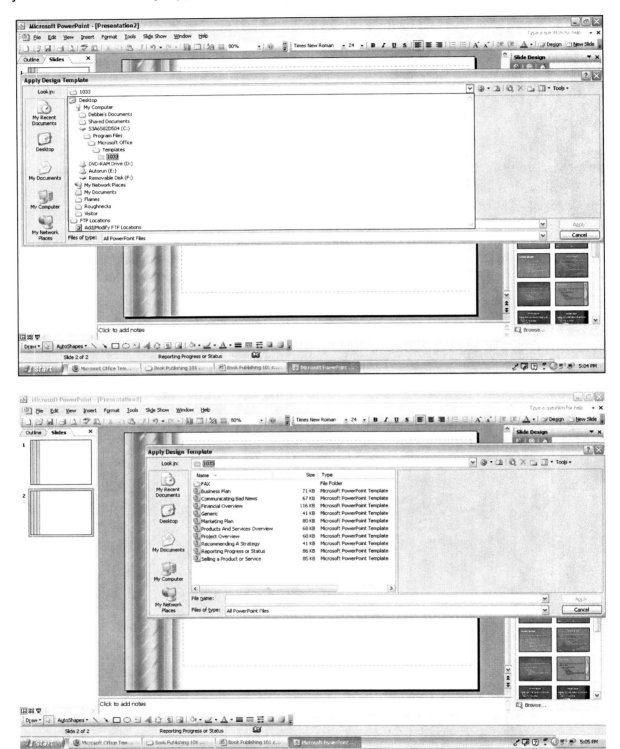

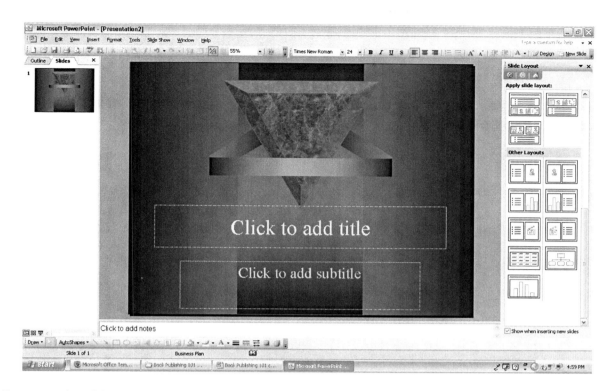

Ideally, you should map out your plan before you start your manuscript. First establish if there is a market. Do your homework. Check Google, Amazon, and Chapters/Indigo for other books written on a similar angle. Plan for sales outside the bookstores. If you get in (and that's a big "if"), consider the bookstores gravy. The rest is your bread and butter.

You also need to know what's out there if you pitch to a traditional publisher. Why should they be interested if there are already other books on the market? Find the unique angle.

Your business plan should factor in timelines for writing, design and layout, printing, distribution, marketing, media, and follow-up. If you have a drop dead date for publication, for example, you want your books ready for a conference, work back from that date. If the conference is December 31 – work back and ask the printer when you need to submit the electronic files to have delivery by the 15th (ideally cushioning for delays like power outages, etc. that could affect the plant). If the printer says November 25, work back two to three weeks, depending on designer's schedule, to allow time for layout. That would mean you must be ready with your edited manuscript by November 4. Always allow for delays. What if you get sick for three days? Factor in major events, work deadlines, and add at least another week for an extra cushion.

Before I began to write Inside the NHL Dream, I produced an outline and laid out a detailed business plan. It included timelines, who I would try and interview, marketing, media campaign, et cetera. I gave myself from September 2001 to February 2002 to gather the interviews for the book. Because I live in Calgary, the Flames were easily accessible but there is a very small window of access to visiting teams. Sometimes, you will not get who you want to interview so you must have a plan B.

In the process of formulating a plan for the next book, I may have the basic goal of what I want it to achieve plus its message so I'll get started in stockpiling research and interview possibilities.

The marketing is a key part of the business plan. Aim for sales outside of bookstores. You'll find some ideas in Step 9 and 10.

Step 4

Sculpting Your Masterpiece

A manuscript is like a sculpture or a painting. You start with that blank slab: the Word page. And then you shape it or sculpt it from there.

Once you start putting those notes in the chapters into action, there are lots of tools.

If you don't have one now, get a good dictionary. Yes, there are online dictionaries. Get a real one – one that is at least 1,500 pages. Regardless of how well you think Spell Check works, using a dictionary to cross reference is the only surefire way to perfection.

Get a comparable thesaurus. I have two. If it's the same size or close to the same size as your dictionary, you won't have any trouble finding replacement words to take out redundancies. You don't want to use the word "said" 1,000 times in one chapter or use the word "report" four times in one paragraph. The computer thesaurus is very limited and only offers a couple of word choices, if any for most words – if it even recognizes the word.

The dictionary and thesaurus are the bread and butter for writing. If you buy no other books, those are the two. When you choose a dictionary, consider the language you will be using the most. There top three dictionaries are Webster's (US), Canadian, and Oxford.

If you're in the market to collect more reference books, there are numerous other dictionaries that cater to urban slang (in various eras), military jargon, politics – name the topic and there is probably a dictionary out there. Some of these dictionaries you can also use online. For instance, even if you want to know what your 14 year old was saying to you in a text message, check out www.urbandictionary.com.

There are other grammar and stylebooks. There are pocket stylebooks that give you a quick reference and there are larger stylebooks or industry-specific stylebooks. If you are ever unsure about a comma or quotation mark, look it up. Sometimes I have to look up the same word or punctuation treatment all the time. They'll help you with everything from using capitalization, how to hyphenate, when to use a comma, colon…anything that has to do with the mechanics of writing. The publishing industry bible is the Chicago Manual of Style.

In the world of text messaging abbreviations, why does it matter that due diligence is the order of the day for grammar? Why does it matter if you may never notice grammar and punctuation in any of the books or articles you've read. It matters when you are sending out a proposal to a publisher. It matters when you are sending out a pitch to write an article for a magazine or newspaper. It matters when you apply for a job. If basic punctuation isn't adhered to in your cover letter, they're going to think, what's the rest of the manuscript look like? What you put out is a reflection of you. Even email. And besides, just because everyone else is doing it, doesn't make it right.

Once you know the rules, it will matter. Once you know the rules, you will see it in those other books, in the magazines and newspapers. You'll be more in tune with it.

Refresher from Lit class

If you were like me, on the day you turned 14, you ran down to the motor vehicle office to apply for your learner's permit. Then as soon as you saved up the money after turning 16, you went for your driver's license. But even when you took your driver's lessons and exam (which was practical application), you thanked your lucky stars that you weren't quizzed academically from the manual you had to read for the learner's permit. In fact, how many of us would even get 50 percent right if we were to take that learner's test today? We've been driving for years, but have developed many habits – some good, some bad – along the way. Driving is like second nature. We don't think about the exact number of feet we're supposed to park from a fire hydrant. We just guess by the look of it. How many can actually see the tires of the vehicle in front while stopped at a light?

Writing is probably the same for most of us, too. Even if we write for a living, the words we use come as second nature. We don't think about subjects and predicates, synonyms or idioms. So for my benefit, as well as yours, here is a list of terminology and lessons we learned in Lit class.

Sentences are made up of a complete idea: a **noun** and a **verb**. A sentence begins with a capital letter and ends with punctuation.

Nouns are people, places, and things, such as a man, tree, chair, and a ball. A **verb** is the action of the noun: a man steers the car; a tree blooms; a chair moves; a ball bounces.

Present tense verb: spitting, writing, walking
Past tense verb: spat, wrote, walked

A **subject** is the main topic of a sentence. A **predicate** describes the subject – it is the action part of the sentence. A <u>tree</u> (noun) <u>blooms</u> (predicate). The <u>squirrel</u> (noun) <u>grabbed the peanut and ran up the tree</u> (predicate).

Synonyms = words that have the same meaning: sunny and bright.

Antonyms = words that are opposite in meaning: night and day.

Homophones = words that sound the same and have different meanings: knight and night.

Contractions = shortening two words by putting them together: don't.

Idiom = figurative expression: in the doghouse.

Dangling modifiers = words or a group of words that do not modify the topic. Wrong: While driving the car, the dog stuck his nose through the open window. Right: While I was driving the car, the dog stuck his nose through the open window. By not putting "I" in the sentence, it sounds like the dog was driving the car.

Things to keep in mind for penning a compelling read

Use an active voice over a passive voice. Passive: Don has been hiding the truth. Active: Don came clean with the truth.

It's Internet, not internet.

Don't misuse pronouns. A company is an "it," not a "they."

Avoid all clichés like the plague.

Avoid dead constructions, such as "There are…"

Begin a sentence with a subject or a verb, rather than a dead construction.

Show and tell the story. Paint a picture with your words.

When possible, use speech to describe your characters' traits.

Hyphens are used to separate compounded words: face-off, self-esteem.

An en dash is used between ranges and values: Anaheim beat Detroit 10–3. The Edmonton–Calgary highway was snow covered this morning.

The em dash can act as a parenthesis or separates related a train of thought: The cats—both belonging to the neighbors—stayed in the yard for most of the day. Katrina skated to a near perfect performance—a school record previously set by Doris.

Some like to put a space on either side of the em dash. Either way is correct.

Some of the editing items to check for:

- ." not ". – This is one of the most common punctuation errors that appears in nearly everything written. The quotation mark *always* comes after the period and the comma, but before the semi-colon, colon, question mark, and exclamation mark.

- % – Unless you are creating an annual report or financial publication where numbers need to stand out, spell out the percentage sign. Whether you use percent or per cent, spell it consistently throughout.

- Twenty-four – If your sentence starts with a number, spell it out. And, when you hyphen a word, if all the words are capitalized in a title, for instance, the second hyphenated word is lower case. I know it looks weird. Look it up.

- Language consistency – Whether you use American, Canadian, or Oxford English, make sure the spelling is consistent throughout.

- Tense consistency – You don't usually use present and past tense in the same narration.

- Spacing after period (one) – This is the next most common error in every manuscript or anything written. Regardless if this is still taught in some circles, two spaces after the period went out when word processing on the computer was invented. It is one space after punctuation – always.

- Consistency in spelling – Check that you've treated a name or spelling the same throughout your manuscript.

- Capitalization – People tend to capitalize words they deem important more than if it is grammatically correct. Proper nouns will name a specific item/person/place and it is capitalized, no matter where it fits in a sentence. Not all words you think are proper nouns are. For instance: Captain Kobe Bryant – the captain is capitalized because it is part of his name. The captain of the basketball team – captain is not capitalized because it is not a proper noun. Other examples: President Barak Obama/the president of the company; the City of New York/the city's homeless; Ottawa City Council/city council members did this; University of Notre Dame/the university students and teachers.

- Explanations if terms are vague – There are some phrases that are generational. We're hearing a little more about the Cold War as Russia and US relations tense again. But don't assume anyone under 30 knows what that is. It goes back to industry jargon. Six-Day War, Cuban Missile Crisis, Jim Crow – a lot of people may not know what that is. Desk encyclopedias are very useful for finding a short description to write.

- Redundancy – Using a thesaurus will help you use different words to say the same thing. Instead of saying "report" three times in one sentence or paragraph, find another word, like "project" or "document," or whatever is applicable.

- Numbering consistency – The rule of thumb is to spell out numbers from one to nine and allow numerical 10 and up. You can also choose to spell out all numbers.

- Commas (serial comma) – The serial comma eliminates any questions about meaning. For example, if my best friend, uncle, sister and husband went shopping, is it my sister's husband or my husband? Without the comma, it's read as my sister's husband. With a comma, it's read as my husband.

  In the book Eats, Shoots & Leaves by Lynne Truss, the title is based on the story of a bear walking into an establishment, eats something, shoots a gun, then goes to walk out. When asked why he did it, he throws a dictionary on the counter and says, "Look it up." In the description, the bear is said to eats, shoots, and leaves instead of eats shoots and leaves.

- Punctuation – When in doubt look it up. There are proper ways to treat punctuation. People tend to use ellipses (…) when a dash is more appropriate. The ellipses actually means there are words missing. Commas can completely change the meaning of a sentence. There are times you can use a colon or semi-colon, and other times when it's not appropriate. A colon would be more appropriate when you plan to add a list, such as: There are three things needed to play backyard football: a field, a pair of runners, and a football. The semi-colon is a bit stronger than a comma and would be used when you separate two complete sentences that are connected in thought or as a comma when listing phrases where commas are used.

- Abbreviations – Spell out abbreviations the first time they are seen in a manuscript. Don't assume others know them. There can be numerous descriptions of the same abbreviation. You would treat it this way: National Football League (NFL). Then after that, you can use the abbreviation throughout the rest of the document.

- Flow – This is something that takes some work. The best way to see flow better is to print off the pages and read it in hard copy.

Language, tense, numbers, and spellings are the biggest areas to look for consistency. Also check the definitions of words, in case you are using the wrong spelling, such as hear and here.

More tips to improve your writing skills

- Don't use a technical word when there is an everyday English equivalent. If your 12 year old cannot understand what you wrote, it's time to rewrite it until he does. Unless you are writing for the academic or computer programming community, the reader will not care how smart you think you are and the technical jargon will both bore them and make them put the book down because they won't understand it.

- Nix the long phrase or word if there is a short one available. Instead of saying "at this point in time," say "now" or another word that describes the moment.

- Clean out extra words. Perhaps the most overused word in the English language is the word "that." If your sentence holds up without it, take it out.

- All right is two words – period!

- Its and it's – if you read out loud "it is" every time you see this, you'll know when to use the apostrophe. The apostrophe represents the word "is." So when it's not there, put the apostrophe in. Its is possessive and doesn't sound right if you read: the dog ate (it is) bone.

- Play. Get creative with descriptive words. Try to paint a picture with emotion. You can get ideas of types of words by using search engines to help. For example, if you want to find ways to hone how people feel about a topic, say their passion for hockey, search: passion, hockey.

Practice your editing skills on email

Regardless of whether an email is personal or business (particularly personal emails at a business location), they are considered a legal document and can be used in court. (Email evidence played a major role in the Enron, WorldCom, and Tyco investigations.) If they are deleted, they can be forensically recovered and would be if a company has been taken to court. That means all those anger emails and off-colored jokes would be included.

There is one way to make sure an email says what is intended to say and there is only one way to do that: RE-READ.

I challenge you to practice your pen skills in every email, whether it's to your mother, sister, or significant other. That means PROOFREADING everything that leaves your computer. How one pens their emails, particularly business emails, can reflect on one's professionalism. When people approach firms for work using the lower case "i" when talking about themselves, perhaps thinking it's cute or they're too lazy to find the shift key, the receiver is likely thinking, 'If that's the effort they put into their work, there is no way I would hire them.'

Nobody is 100 percent perfect. You may even find the odd error in this workbook, but I can assure you it has been proofed, re-proofed, printed off, and proofed again, several times. Those who do the due diligence to ensure their emails read as well as any written letter mailed set themselves ahead of pretty much 90 percent of the pack. It's also good practice that translates to penning your manuscript.

More sculpting

Once you get the meat of your material together, you have to print it off. That's when some of the little misses jump off the page. You can also see the flow of the document much better.

Flow is how the paragraphs meld into each other – how the chapters mesh together. A good way to check the flow of a sentence is to read it aloud. If you stumble on the words, it might be a sign to rewrite it so it will flow off your tongue better.

You can always improve a sentence. There isn't just one correct way but by looking at the examples, you can see how you can make your sentences crisper and easier to read.

(I'm Not Drunk, I'm Disabled by Cory Johnson, http://www.coryjohnson.ca/)

Before:

One of Cory's favourite hobbies was taking in a good Calgary flames hockey game. Every year during the playoffs, Calgary's 17th ave. turns into the red mile after the Calgary flames win. The red mile is flooded with energetic fans, some with questionable sobriety. Cory's personal experiences have told or shown him that he looked and sounded like he was intoxicated or drunk. Cory often found himself being teased and harassed by drunken individuals because of it. He thinks this is because an intoxicated person usually becomes intimidated by someone who appears drunker than they are!

After:

A favorite hobby of mine is taking in a good Calgary Flames hockey game. That includes the Red Mile.

Every year during the playoffs, Calgary's 17th Avenue becomes the Red Mile after a win. It is flooded with energetic fans, some with questionable sobriety. My personal experiences have shown me that I look and sound like I'm intoxicated or drunk. Teasing and harassment by some of these drunken individuals happens because of it. Maybe it is because an intoxicated person usually becomes intimidated by someone who appears drunker than they are.

(http://www.cplseminars.com/)

Before:

In this one day "Stress in Check" seminar you will gain the knowledge to untangle the mystery of *Stress* which will bring clarity to the management of it.

"Stress in Check" is a Constructive Progressive Learning Seminar Event that looks at *Stress* management from a <u>unique point of view</u>. Although we all differ in appearance, in our responsibilities, upbringings, families, opinions, beliefs and work conditions, we are more similar than different. Our bodies and minds are structured in much the same way and that includes our <u>ability to think</u>. We are all "Human Beings" and

our basic cycle of learning, which is associated to thinking, <u>is wired much the same way</u>. It is just the outcome of our thinking that differs.
After:

In this one day "Stress in Check" seminar, you will untangle the mystery of stress and gain clarity for the management of it.

"Stress in Check" is a Constructive Progressive Learning Seminar Event that looks at stress management from a unique point of view. We may all differ in appearance, responsibility, upbringing, family, opinion, belief, and work conditions, but our bodies and minds are structured in much the same way – including our ability to think.

Some words are confusing. When in doubt, look it up.

This is a true story. I was penning an article about a housing development and the term palette was used with respect to the array of colors available for home exteriors. The client asked me to double check the spelling. If we weren't confused before, here was what I uncovered from the *Webster's New World Dictionary, Third College Edition*:

- *Palate:* roof of mouth, sense of taste
- *Palette:* thin board or tablet of wood, plastic, often with hole at one end for thumb; arranges and mixes paint; the colors used by a particular artist for painting
- *Pallet:* wooden tool consisting of flat blade with handle; small bed or pad filled with straw; vertical stripe half as wide as a pale
- *Palette:* low, portable platform, in which materials are stacked
- *Pallette:* plate protecting the armpit

Which phrase is wrong or are they both right?

Women's rights	Womens' rights
Teachers College	Teacher's College
Cold roast beef	Cold, roast, beef
Re-evaluate	Reevaluate
Anti-Israeli	Anti Israeli
She was a 12-year-old girl.	She was a 12 year old girl.
He was 18 years old.	He was 18-years-old.
Gen. George Custer	Gen. Custer
Rev. Jessie Jackson	Rev. Jackson
He was all right.	He was alright.
Enthusiastic	Enthuse
First, he opened the drawer. Second, he took out a pen.	Firstly, he opened the drawer. Secondly, he took out a pen.
My best friend and I met at the bar.	My best friend and me met at the bar.
Craig called Sheri and me over to the bench.	Craig called Sheri and I over to the bench.
The trophy was presented to both my protégé and me.	The trophy was presented to both my protégé and myself.
My partner and I headed for the exit.	My partner and myself headed for the exit.
The car was parked alongside the driveway.	The car was parked along side of the driveway.
It's not the way it should be done.	Its not the way it should be done.

Hint: the phrase on the left is correct.

When you're stuck

Numerous exercises in books and magazines can help you get unstuck. Check out Writer Magazine and Writer's Digest.

There are a lot of tools to guide you through and get you into the zone.

Writing a manuscript doesn't have to be done all in one shot. You can write one chapter at a time, the whole book at a time. You can write the ending before the beginning. Sometimes you don't have the research to do it at the same time.

One thing I can tell you for sure. What you put into the words on the page is what the reader gets out of it. Imagine going to the concert of your favorite singer and he/she comes out to sing two songs, then walks off the stage as it that were enough. That person might think that's all you need because you paid to see them and hear them sing. You might have spent $150 a ticket. Yes, you did see them and you did hear them sing, but what is your perceived value of the performance?

In a true-life example of this, I used to sell tickets for a box office in Edmonton, Alberta, and in the case of two concerts: Aretha Franklin and Gladys Knight and the Pips, they each had half a room filled – Aretha at the Jubilee Auditorium (2,727 capacity) and Knight at the Coliseum (17,353). Both of them walked off the stage after about two songs and the box office had to refund the tickets. They never returned to the city and I've never thought much of them since.

On the flip side, Frankie Valli was the ultimate professional. I went to his concert in Edmonton at the Coliseum some time in the early 1980s. There were 1,000 people in a 17,000+-seat arena. He called everyone to come and sit up close, then performed as if he had a full house. Everyone raved about his concert and class. When he re-booked Edmonton a year later, he had a full house at the Jubilee Auditorium. I've seen some discussion on a professional speaker newsletter about what to do if organizers say to expect an audience of 400 people and less than 50 show up. If you perform like Frankie Valli, the ones who show up will become your biggest disciples.

Don't you feel the reader is going to feel ripped off if you didn't work at making the manuscript the best it could be through research and editing?

Yes, it's hard. I don't know where anyone ever said writing was easy. When you throw the words on the page, that isn't the end. You shape it, sculpt it, and keep going at it until you can finally let it go. Sometimes you're so sick of editing that the last thing you want to do is re-read it again. People do see the effort. They appreciate it. It makes it easier for them.

It's like being a professional athlete. When you see Sidney Crosby top the National Hockey League scoring and breaking records, he didn't just step on the ice when he was drafted. He started at a very young age, was a rink rat, shooting pucks for hours after practice. He continually worked at improving his weaknesses. That's what we have to do if we want to be taken seriously as a writer – improve our weaknesses, which nine times out of 10 is editing.

It doesn't mean your manuscript or completed book will be perfect. But if there is a mistake in there, the reader is more likely to overlook it because they see the effort you put into the rest of the book. Everyone who works on a book from author to publisher to graphic designer is human. The goal is to eliminate errors through exhaustive editing.

There's no easy way of doing it. Think of it like deciding one morning that you want to become an actor. You can go to Universal Studios tomorrow to enter a cattle call for a blockbuster movie by Steven Spielberg. What do you think your chances will be? Unless you have the right look or happen to be naturally gifted, you have to work at it and take acting lessons.

In writing, you can learn from other projects, get a little creative. The first thing you can do right now is practice on your emails. Read your emails. How many people re-read their emails before they send them out? See what comes into your inbox to know what your email looks like when it goes to someone else's.

Put a project together with your kids. It doesn't have to be 300 pages, it can be 10. It can be a collaborative effort. You can both work the flow and other elements together.

You don't have to do it alone. You can collaborate with a friend or colleague. You can do one page, send it to someone else to do the second page; you get it back to do the third page, and so on. You can do a book in pictures. The key is just to do it.

How do you know when you're ready and what risk is there to being ready?

Everyone has their own area of readiness. Much of it might depend on what you intend to do with your manuscript. When people have been ready, it's done. They can sit on it for years.

The fear of the risk or the unknown may be part of the procrastination. If you do the due diligence to back up your sources and write with a purpose, your manuscript will be fine. If you're writing an exposé book with the intention of sensationalism or to hurt someone, you need a lawyer. You can use real life examples of situations that were dicey – just change the names and the environment so no one can pinpoint the tale back to the actual person or event. It's about the journey of the story – not the details.

In the interviews, when you develop a relationship, you will talk off topic, even though some of that will be on tape. You must decide if that off topic material – however good it may be – is worth using if it will make that interviewee uncomfortable or cause them harm.

But when you are ready, wild horses won't stop you.

Places to write or express your mind

- Social networks
- Blogs and Ezines
- Newsletters
- Your website
- Leave meaty tips in discussion boards
- Create YouTube videos
- iTunes
- Flickr

Go and find your voice

Writing is akin to method acting. Before the writer can render a fully convincing world, he must inhabit that world and every major character that lives there.
Richard North Patterson – No Safe Place

Be meticulous in your proofing. Don't let anything leave your possession until you know it's your best work.

Michael Jordan glided to the basket without effort. The good writer seems to communicate without exertion.

Grow a thick skin.

Really mean every word you write.

Step 5

Dispelling the Myths of Traditional Publishing

Types of publishing

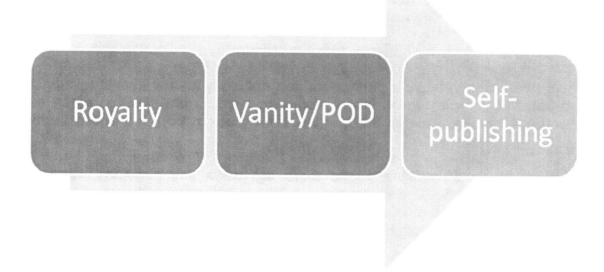

How do you find a publisher?

A royalty publisher is a firm that takes on the rights to publish a book and offers the author a royalty payment: a percentage of the sale of the book.

But first, I want to throw in some facts here about the publishing industry that you might not want to know.

Why publishing a book is so difficult?

- Few unsolicited manuscripts are read
- Publishers are driven by a vision, not unsolicited material
- Editors look for average writers who are experts in a subject area
- Only the decision making editor and publisher's ideas and wants get published
- Often, good unsolicited ideas are assigned to other writers
- Publishers want writers who help them achieve their own vision of what they want their books to be

By the way, besides book publishing, this formula is the same for writing articles for publications.

So why is this so difficult? One of the reasons for is this. My royalty publisher, Self-Counsel Press, told me that for the 30 titles it produces each year, it receives 2,500 pitches. If you do the math and take one of the larger publishers that produce 100 to 150 titles a year, they probably get 5,000 to 6,000 applicants for those titles annually. This is why it may seem easier to get an audience with the Pope.

Getting an agent is even more difficult. There are few publishers that offer advances and the agent works on a percentage of the advance and sales. Most agents will only work with authors who are already published. Because it's all a numbers' game, they sometimes will look at the profile of the author first. It doesn't matter how great you think your manuscript is, they view it with their own eyes.

The publisher does want to be your partner and it is not really an adversarial relationship. They do want to uphold their own vision when producing a book, however, so when soliciting a publisher, you need to always keep this in mind. **It isn't about you, it's about them and the reader.**

There are ways to solicit publishers and there are ways you shouldn't. Here are some examples of what NOT to do. These are real emails. I'm not making this up. Also note that the intention is not to mock these emails. They may very well be excellent projects, but no one will ever give them a serious look because of the first impression.

Looking for a publicher

This fellow sent an email in a grouping, where every email address in Association of Canadian Publishers Directory was listed. He also attached the full manuscript.

> Looking_for _a _publ isher.pdf
> Looking for a publicher
>
> Estimable Sir
>
> I wrote two books in informatics. I think that these are good and I send to you the cover, the contents and a paragraph from everyone. If you are interested, please answer to me for sending the entire fist form for every book. Everyone has a CD with the application programs, whose design was performed in the books. I trust in you, for helping me. See attachments. No viruses.
>
> the authOr.

Gula and Kolya

This email was also sent to group but the emails were hidden. This manuscript was also attached.

> I am writing in the hope that you will be interested in reading my book, "Brothers." It is a picture book for a broad audience and tells the story of Gula and Kolya, dogs with very different personalities. I think this might be a good fit for your list.
>
> I hope this will be of interest to you. Please see "Brothers" attached.

Dire Wolf Lycans are not evil

This email was sent the same way the previous one.

Hello,My name is EriC. I am a new Horror story writer I have been working on a Book Trilogy for the last Couple of years and have completed book 1 .
The name of my book is TommyBoy.
This is a brief outline of the Legacy of TommyBoy .
The story is about two different breeds of Lycans.(Lycans are a form of werewolf) Decended from a common ancestor

The Dire Wolf Lycans are not evil.

Rath Lycans are evil,And want to control the world.
Enslave mankind and kill
all Dire Wolf Lycans

The story follows a Lycan family that for generations has been guarding the Sacred Items of The Lycans. The Lycan Prophacy says that a very powerful child will be born from good and evil.He is the Chosen One. As the time of his birth draws near the world will wittness THe Begining Of The End

This email goes on and on, and then he says

BOOK 1 Tells the story of the West family and there struggles to stay alive as the Rath Lycans destroy the world. Book 1 will cover all events leading up to the birth of The Chosen One
Book 2 Will deal with the next 18 years of The Chosen Ones Life and his struggle to stay alive in a frozen world locked in a nucular winter.
Book 3 Will deal with the final battle .The Battle For Mankind.

This is a very graphic book ,Violently and ~exually Graphic.
I am looking for a publisher who is willing to give a 1 st time writer a chance.
Currently i am just about finished my second book that is titled HeliGate.

I am very eager to get working on the second book In the TommyBoy Trilogy

As i am new to writing my book will need some editing",Would your company be interested in publishing my books. Thak you ,Eric
I am a new face in the horror writing industry. I have been published in Buckmasters hunting Magazines many times.Im looking for a dedicated publisher who is willing to edit and publish my many new books that will be
forthcoming over the next couple of years.My books are very raw and graphic in nature,As there is a new generation of readers out there who crave more from books as well as movies.1 hope your company is willing to become my publisher as i can guarentee, If you can publish and market my books that you will find a big fan

PS I ALSO AM CONTACTING SEVERAL SCRIPT WRITERS FOR USA MOVIE PRODUCTIONS

Good Book

This email was also grouped and in the body of the email, he included his photograph.

> Subject: Good Book
>
> Attachment: ███████ Stick.doc (908 KB)
> Dear Literary Agent, Dear Publisher,
>
> My name is ██████████, and I am an Italian writer. It is an honour for me to send you a piece of my work entitled: "████████ Stick". It consists of a collection of short stories and aphorisms, based on the zen style, and it has already been published in Italy, obtaining a good number of sales.
>
> If you are interested in my work, as I hope you are, you might like to know that a second volume of such work is already available and has not been published in Italy yet. It would be a pleasure for me to collaborate with you for our mutual economic and moral satisfaction.
>
> Yours faithfully,

If you list the entire directory's addresses in the "To" section of the email, the subject line says looking for a publisher, and there is also an attachment, what do you think your chances of getting a publisher are?

If you are going to look for a publisher please, if you don't do anything else at least go to its Website. If you want to know who publishes children's books go to the association directory, where there is a list of all the member publishers and a blurb on what the publisher publishes. Then you can go directly onto the individual websites and figure out if these publishers would consider publishing the book that you've written, if a similar book has already been published, or if that publisher targets a specific genre of that audience. You need to find out if there's a fit before you actually send anything.

Publishers will not accept unsolicited manuscripts under any circumstances, and most publishers, even in today's world of email and social networking, about 80 percent of them do not accept email queries. You have to mail in your query letter. To learn how a publisher wants to receive inquiries, or if it will even consider one, look at its submission guidelines. There are a few publishers that do not accept any submissions. That doesn't mean they don't accept new projects; it just means they prefer dealing with an agent.

In your query letter, you would include your outline, a simplified outline. If you do get in the door and they do want more information, then they will ask you for it. You approach them with at least knowing what they publish – to see if it's a fit, otherwise it's a waste of their time, of your time.

However, most of us, and even those who have a few manuscripts under our belts, have done all this before: making several copies of the manuscript and mailing them out to every publisher under the sun. All it did was cost a whole lot on photocopying and postage.

It's not about you and how good you think your manuscript is. It's about them.

Here's another story of how someone might get caught up in their manuscript's importance. A woman I know who runs a company that provides volunteers for special events, such as golf tournaments and fundraising dinners, received an email from a fellow who said he was single starving author who hoped one day to be a single published author. He was looking for the services of several volunteers to help turn his dream into reality and asked if he had come to the right place by contacting her. She prompted him further to explain what it was he actually needed. He replied he was looking to get a publisher for book, and because he expected it would make millions of dollars, he needed volunteers in several cities to help market his book. Of course, she passed him off to me to respond.

How the bookselling industry works

How book profits work

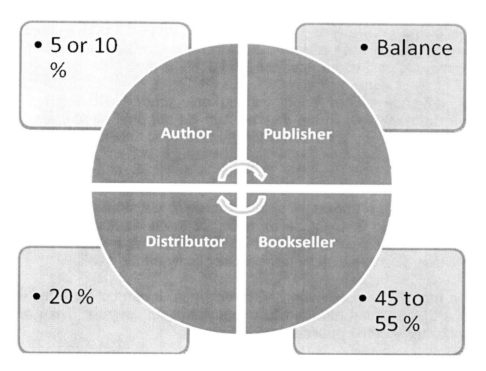

It's a somewhat dysfunctional business model where nobody really benefits.

To give you an idea of how the industry works, as I mentioned earlier, there is a lot of competition for very few spots to get published. Just doing the cover letter, outline, checking out the publisher first, adhering to the submission guidelines will help you get to maybe the top 20 percent of the slush pile.

The publishing industry works this way: the publisher publishes a book. In royalty publishing, the author writes the book, sells it to the publisher, which entails turning his or her rights over to the publisher for a period of time – two years is usually the norm before the rights revert back to the author. That's the price you pay to have somebody else publish your book. You need to make sure those rights revert back to you. When the book has worn out its shelf life, you get the rights to publish *your* book back in your lap, then you can take it and publish it elsewhere or publish it yourself.

Royalty fees vary amongst publishers, but generally it's 10 percent to the author. Whatever the retail cost of the book, 10 percent of that goes back into the author's jeans. Now in the case of my Self-Publishing 101 book, I received 10 percent for Canadian sales and only five percent of American sales. Considering the book is selling in the US at least six to one, with only five percent royalties, I'm more able to buy a few cups of Starbucks rather than a new house.

The royalty aspect of a book is not going to make you rich if you are the author. Not every publisher will offer an advance, either. There are fewer and fewer advances being paid out.

The advance is really this. You are actually borrowing money against the royalties of the book. If the publisher is giving you, say a $2,000 advance, that's $2,000 against the 10 percent royalties that you are getting back after the books are sold. The good news is if there aren't enough sales to cover the cost of the advance, you don't have to give the money back.

Chances are the advance money might be the only money you receive from the book, depending on how the book sells in the market. And it's not paid all at once. You would get a portion of the advance up front; a portion after the book is completed; and a portion after it is out in the marketplace.

The shelf life for books isn't that long, either. I've been told by a major book chain that the typical shelf life of a book in a bookstore is about three to six months, unless it's selling. For a picture book or fiction book, it might be as soon as three weeks. If you've ever been in a bookstore or sat and had a coffee in the bookseller's coffee bar and watched the people going up and down the aisles, you see exactly how fast books fly off the shelf.

That leads to the big "R" in publishing: the return ratio. It can be quite high – more than 50 percent. Returns are not books returned to a bookstore for refunds. They are unsold books returned to the publisher – at the publisher's expense.

So if 10 percent of the retail cost goes the author, 20 percent usually goes to the distributor. The distributor is the middleman between the publisher and bookstore – if the book gets in the bookstore.

The booksellers use a distributor because there are so many publishers. If everybody you know is a publisher and they all went to the bookstore all at the same time, the bookseller is not going to want to talk to everybody. The distributor will act as the go-between. It would put the publishers' books in its catalogue and deal directly with the bookstore. For the distributors' role, it takes 20 percent. It also provides the fulfillment. The publisher would send its books to the distributor, which in turns markets the books to the bookstores.

That said, the booksellers basically look through the catalogue and choose their books based on their own interest. The same chain store in the east may not buy the same books as a chain store in the west. It's much like the fashion industry, when the buyers head over to Europe six months in advance to figure out what the North American market will buy.

The bookstore cut varies between 45 to 55 percent between retail and online bookstores. Amazon and Borders take 55 percent, and some retail bookstores take 45 percent. As a publisher, by the time you get your money out of the retail cost, you're getting about 30 percent.

Here's another myth: just because a publisher – large or small – has published your book, it does not mean your book is going to get into a bookstore. The bookstore buyer flips through that list of books in a catalogue and says, I'll take one of those. Your book may never get into a bookstore. It has to appeal to the buyer. I know of a couple of royalty published authors who cannot get their books in a bookstore. Not only can't they get their books in the bookstore, they can't get their books listed on the *bookseller's* Internet site.

That's the down side of the royalty publishing industry. The upside is you're using someone else's money to publish a book. You don't usually have control over design, layout, or distribution and sometimes have to fight for editorial, but the publisher will eat all the costs of production.

Once accepted by a royalty publisher – With getting a publisher, you have to negotiate contracts. They're not necessarily written in favor the author. They're mostly standard, but you can negotiate a contract through a lawyer, agent, or even through yourself, if you know what you're doing.

In return for allowing a publisher to publish your book, you are letting them borrow the rights to do so for a certain period of time, usually two years. After that, the rights revert back to you – and this should be in writing. It's probably the most important aspect of the contract. This is what print on demand firms (who are NOT royalty publishers) have sleuthed and held authors hostage over. (See archived articles at www.writersweekly.com.)

Once you get your book accepted by a traditional publisher, there is some back and forth on the editorial. You don't usually get to give a lot of feedback on the design and layout itself, but sometimes you have to negotiate on the editorial. In one instance, a manuscript's editing process was completed and both the author and publisher were satisfied with the product. The publisher put out a review sample copy of the book and sent it to the author, who saw the publisher had changed one word throughout the entire book, which changed its entire meaning. Fortunately, the publisher changed it back when the author asked it to.

You can keep your book on the shelf longer when you're active in marketing. But as an author, whether you self-publish or royalty publish, you always have to take a very proactive role in selling your books.

The royalty publisher basically throws it in a catalogue. If your publisher does 150 titles, unless your book falls into the top 10 percent of what it thinks are going to be bestsellers, your book will just sit in the catalogue. Publishers try to figure out which books are going to be big sellers and that's what they put their marketing dollars behind. You can influence that if you have a very strong marketing plan in the first place – when you send in the proposal.

Regardless if royalty or self-published:

An aggressive author = getting noticed = sales = longer shelf life

Authors are in partnership with the publisher. You don't just sit back and wait for the publisher to sell books, because in most cases, it won't.

In royalty publishing, you don't have control over pricing or distribution. Self-publishers can set a price for bulk sales and have control over how books are distributed. For instance, if an association wanted to use a book as a textbook or make copies available for its members and if they wanted to buy a few hundred copies, as a self-publisher, you can decide on a special bulk discount in order to insure sales. If an association wanted to buy a thousand books, you could do a specialized printing and even personalize a page because you get them to cover the cost of printing. I call it the Wal-Mart factor – sell more for less than less the more. But with royalty publishing, a lot of times the publisher won't budge on the discount.

Authors generally get 10 free books from the publisher and the rest you have to buy back for the same discount as the booksellers.

This is not to say it's a bad experience to go royalty. You would have a good partner that has the expertise, a lot of people in-house, lawyers and everything else you need to move you through the manuscript with relative ease. These are all things that you would have to pay out of pocket for as a self-publisher. The process can be longer than self-publishing, but it can be a very nice partnership.

Step 6

When to Publish the Book Yourself

So what are the advantages of self-publishing? I can think of one thing: control. You have control over everything: layout, editorial, price, distribution, bulk sales, and marketing.

There is still an opportunity to get it into bookstores and into the same distribution chains if you're self-published.

You might have heard of these authors and book titles:

- Virginia Woolf (who, with her husband, ran a publishing house that produced books by other authors as well as her own), Rudyard Kipling, D.H. Lawrence, and Zane Grey, to name a few, self-published.
- Mark Twain self-published *The Adventures of Huckleberry Finn* because he had issues with his previous publishers. The proceeds from the book helped him fund the development of one of the first working typewriters.
- Leo Tolstoi paid 4,500 rubles to publish his first novel, *War and Peace.*
- Edgar Allen Poe self-published some of his work.
- Tom Peters self-published *In Search of Excellence* and sold more than 25,000 copies in the first year. After that, he sold the rights to a conventional publisher.
- With his friends' help, James Joyce paid for the 1922 printing of *Ulysses.*
- Howard Fast's involvement in the Communist Party made publishers leery, so he published *Spartacus* himself in 1951.
- *The Tale of Peter Rabbit* was self-published by author Beatrix Potter after it was initially rejected by a publisher afraid of the illustration costs. The publisher then changed its mind in 1902 after seeing the self-published version and thought about the commercial possibilities. The book has subsequently sold over 40 million copies and was translated into 35 languages.
- Irma Rombauer used $3,000 of her own money to publish *The Joy of Cooking* in 1931.
- George Bernard Shaw self-published some of his writings before he became famous.
- Nathaniel Hawthorne, who wrote *The House of the Seven Gables* and *The Scarlet Letter,* self-published his first book.
- Ernest Hemingway and T.S. Eliot self-published their first books.
- James Redfield sold 80,000 copies of *The Celestine Prophecy* from the trunk of his car before it sold to a conventional publisher.
- Walt Whitman self-published some of his poems.
- Deepak Chopra vanity-published his first book before selling the rights to a traditional publisher, where it became one of his bestsellers.
- Benjamin Franklin used the pen name Richard Saunders to self-publish *Poor Richard's Almanack* in 1732.
- Dave Chilton self-published *The Wealthy Barber.*
- Richard Nixon self-published *Real Peace.*
- Ken Blanchard and Spencer Johnson initially self-published *The One-Minute Manager.* Experts told them they would never sell a short book for $15. It took them three months to sell over 20,000 copies in San Diego alone.

A publisher came knocking at these authors' doors once they sold several thousands of their self-published books. One of the reasons why a person would consider that is fulfillment. Unless you have paid staff to carry out the distribution, that could probably wear you down.

But for others, they will self-publish because they have a message they want to share with others and it is the easiest and fastest way to do it. As you learned in Step 5, finding a royalty publisher is extremely difficult. Many publishers are set in their ways and don't venture outside of the traditional box when it comes to editorial content.

Another reason people will self-publish is to keep the money for themselves. You receive 100 percent of the proceeds, even though you incur 100 percent of the costs.

In self-publishing, you can test the waters, try something new, use unconventional methods to market. The sky is the limit.

But – and this is a big but – just because a book is self-published does not mean it has to LOOK self-published.

Step 7

The First Step in Producing a Professional Product:
Getting Your Book to Layout

Using ISBNs, Cataloguing in Print numbers, and barcodes will elevate your book's credibility. The ISBN is a book's DNA. Regardless of where you reside, it is a unique number and recognized worldwide.

Bowker (www.bowker.com) is the American distributor for ISBNs. It's unclear whether it is a branch of the government or if it a private business. You can buy ISBNs individually (starting at $125) or in clusters (blocks of 10, 100, or 1,000 from $400 to $1,875). Bowker also distributes barcodes.

In Canada, the ISBN is government issued (www.collectionscanada.gc.ca). You would apply online as a publisher, and the process usually takes a couple of days. Once you receive a user login, the rest is up to the publisher. Getting an ISBN is instant. It's a great system and requires little manpower for the ISBN office administration. The publisher is able to update the status of each release.

Internationally, you can find a link to one of the 160 ISBN agencies worldwide here: http://www.isbn-international.org/.

A Cataloguing in Print number puts your book into the national library catalogue. The National Library of Canada publicizes new publications throughout library system through ISBN numbers and through Government of Canada's Website. In the US, you would apply for a CIP number through the Library of Congress (www.loc.gov).

In the US, you can get the barcode when you apply for the ISBN. In Canada, there are a couple of places to receive barcodes, but most certainly one of the reputable locations is Barcode Graphics (www.barcodegraphics.com). You would only apply for a barcode account if you intend on producing several books each month. Otherwise, you can a book printer can insert one at the time of printing.

Book format

The Chicago Manual of Style lays out all the elements of the book format and explains exactly what each of the items are. The title page is the first thing you see when you open up the book. The copyright page is where you have the ISBN, library catalog number, and information about the publisher.

Here is a template for the order of sections in a typical book.

- Title page: might include just the title and author; can include edition and publisher

- Copyright page: publishing information, ISBN, CIP, copyright holder, year...

- Reviews: may or may not be included in a book; this is where you commonly see them

- Dedication

- Table of contents

- Foreword

- Introduction

- Other front matter: might include map (such as in military planning), list of abbreviations, etc.

- Chapters

- Conclusion, Afterword, Epilogue

- Appendixes: explanations and/or elaborations of chapter material

- Chronology

- Endnotes

- Glossary

- Bibliography or references

- List of contributors

- Index

If a book is hardcover, then it is common to have the author information on the cover wrap. Otherwise, if a book is soft cover, the author information might be on the back cover or inside, after the conclusion.

You could have a couple blank pages in front. Some will have testimonials in the front. As for your copyright page, where the ISBN and publisher information is, it should always sit on the left-hand side. It doesn't really matter if testimonials are ahead of the title page. But the title page would come before the copyright page. If you ever have any questions about layout, just go to the books on your shelf. They're usually all in the same type of format.

Finding a graphic designer

In choosing a graphic designer, it's important to feel confident that that person will honor your vision and not just hear what you say and then do their own thing. You want them to be able to incorporate their creative elements, but include your vision for the book.

They need to know what the book is about in as much detail as possible. They tend not to read the material, rather just focus on the overall outline and basic gist of the book.

But before you get a graphic designer, you need to make sure they work in a program that speaks to the printer's requirements. It helps if you get the designer and the printer's tech support staff to speak directly to each other so there is no miscommunication.

Your manuscript should be done in Word. Regardless if the designer is working in a PC or Mac, Word is universal and will flow through a layout program with relative ease.

Microsoft Publisher is great for doing up your own marketing materials and dressing up files, but it is not compatible with most printers. It will cost you several dollars more for the printer to make the files compatible, and you'll probably have several layout errors and issues that come about as a result. Printer programs don't work very well with Word either.

That's not to say there won't be errors. It's inevitable. But you will minimize them and the printer may also be able to make changes effortlessly with compatible source files, such as InDesign, PageMaker, and Quark Express. Any questions about how a printer needs to receive the files should be addressed directly with the printer.

Graphic designers must:

- Speak the same format language the printer requires the files to be in
- Be sensitive to your needs as an author for vision, style, look, costs, and timeline
- Be flexible to revise layout as needed
- Work with the printer to ensure files are trouble-free for printing

But how do you actually find a designer? You can ask the printer. You can look online by Googling graphic designers in whatever city/town you live in and check out your center's online directories. You could try educational institutes that offer graphic design programs. Any marketing/advertising agency can also do the job. You could go to a print on demand service, but really check them out first. Even some of the so-called reputable POD firms have a good share of horror stories, where clients wait for months on end to receive their book or have their corrections done, or are held hostage over being able to retrieve the files they have already paid for.

Professionals will charge a variety of rates. Cheaper is not necessarily lesser quality and more expensive is not necessarily better. You want to see a portfolio of their creativeness, whether it includes other books or not. You can get a good feel as to how clean and crisp their layout might be, based on some of their other work. If they have worked on annual reports, they can work on book layouts. It is the same process.

You want to feel like the graphic designer understands how you might like your book to look. Find some of your own examples to help show what you mean. Give the designer a good overview of what your book is about and who your target reader is. For example, if your target readers are seniors, you might want to consider larger and cleaner fonts, such as 12-point Arial, Tahoma, or Verdana. The more you can share about what your vision is, the more likely the designer will nail it on their first attempt. Also, the less time your designer spends on your book, the less it will cost.

Design quirks to look out for that impact the professional look of your book

Just because it seems every royalty-published book on the shelf doesn't adhere to some of the following elements, does not mean they are right. I guarantee if you pay attention to these items, your book will look better than most other books. You will raise eyebrows when you exceed your peers' expectation as to how they thought your self-published book will look.

Keep your reader in mind when you are doing a layout. If your audience is over 30, chances are they will not enjoy a 10-point font. The type of font will also impact the ease of navigation for a reader.

Personally, I prefer a sans serif font, as opposed to a serif font. I find they make the text flow easier and my eyes don't tire as easily. Using a sans serif font, coupled with spacing in between paragraphs, makes the reading experience even easier. The next time you pick up a serif font book (usually Times New Roman) with indented paragraphs stuck together, see how easy it is to find your place when you have to put the book down in comparison. The layout of an instructional book is even more important for making it visually appealing.

Serif font examples:
Times New Roman
Adobe Garamond Pro
Century Schoolbook
Garamond
Palatino

Sans serif font examples:
Arial
Calibri
Franklin Gothic Book
Helvetica
Tahoma
Verdana

Images

They must be higher resolution. That includes graphs and charts. You can't just cut and paste them from a Word file or low resolution into a book layout. They need to be at least 300 dpi for them to print well.

Hyphenation

Please, please, please tell the designer to TURN OFF the hyphenation. Otherwise words will hyphenate where they don't need to be. It is annoying to the reader when every other word is hyphenated. I've seen five-letter words hyphenated onto the next page.

Widows and orphans

These are dangling sentences at the top and bottom of a page that belong to a paragraph on the next page and tiny words that sit alone on the next line. In order to line up the opposing pages top and bottom, the graphic designer would play with the spacing between the paragraphs.

Times New Roman

Please, it is NOT the only font on the planet. Just because it is the default font in every program does not mean you have to use it.

Indented paragraphs and no spacing in between

It is harder to find your place when you put the book down plus it seems to be the same layout in every single book in the universe. Add space between the paragraphs, whether you indent or not.

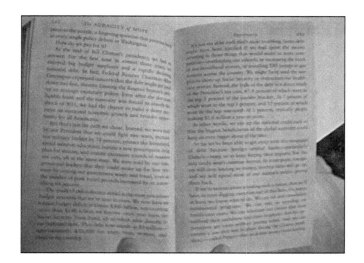

Weird stuff

It is one space after period, not two; check for funny PC or MAC stuff; check for return/end paragraph, for example:

> *Do search and replace on spaces. You might have to do this two or three times until you get rid of all extra spaces*

Fonts

These need to be included if uploading the source files to printer. Fonts are licensed.

So while you may have edited the manuscript several times before it went to layout, you still need to edit it again after layout, in particular, looking out for some of these issues.

With layouts, you'll likely have to print it off and mark up the pages, then send the pages to the designer. You won't be able to change the electronic files. The graphic designer will have to physically input the changes.

Word templates

There several Word book templates available online, but many of the sites will charge you for them. Some of the prices I've seen range around $35 to $39. If you search hard enough, you may find free templates available. However, what you'll need to do is once you've done your manuscript in Word, you need to save it in a PDF before sending it to a printer. You'll only be able to get a decent printing if it's digital processing rather than offset, because Word isn't a high enough resolution. This is probably the most economic way to produce a layout, but you are limited to what you can do for formatting. You want to also take this Word file through the same layout editing process mentioned earlier. This workbook was produced in Word on purpose. So you can compare this to a book done by a professional graphic designer using InDesign or another layout program.

Turn off hyphenation (tell the designer this when they get the file – it's annoying to the reader)

Check for funny PC to MAC stuff (i.e. instead of quotation mark, it shows something like this: ⬜)

Check for return/end paragraphs

Check for spacing issues; such as too much in between words if text is full-justified and spacing between paragraphs

Step 8

The Final Product

Two types of publishing

To simplify, digital printing works similar to your laser printer. It prints books a page at a time. When you send a digital printer the layout files, you don't have to worry about page counts because it prints individual pages. Of course, the number of pages goes into the cost of your quote.

Digital is great when you're printing small runs. You're paying a little bit more per unit but you can print as few as one book. The more you print, the less cost per unit. Once you start getting to 750 to 1,000 books, that's when digital printing starts to become more expensive. Then you want to look into offset printing.

You would only go offset if you are printing a higher quantity of books or if image quality is important. Pictures turn out better in offset. Your unit cost is going to be much better. The setup costs for offset is considerably higher than digital. This is where you need to take page counts into consideration. You need to find out from the printer how many pages make up a signature.

A signature represents a flat sheet that has pages of the book printed on both sides. Then the signature is folded and trimmed and set into the binding. If you've seen binding get old and brittle on some older books, pages fall out in clumps rather than a page at a time – this is a signature. If you look closely at the spine of an offset book, you can actually see the page groupings.

A book might be eight pages to a signature. Sometimes it's more. Sometimes it varies. You need to have a conversation with the printer with respect to what the layout page count is and what the page count would be on the signatures. If your book falls a few pages under the signature, you then make the decision to allow the extra blank pages at the back or trim pages off the book to fit the signature. That's why you see blank pages at the back of some books. Some people will print "notes" at the top; some leave it blank. Those are pages that make up the signature.

If you're one page over, unless you remove a page somewhere or add some, you're printing a whole signature for one page. That isn't very cost effective as your unit cost per book goes up for each signature.

The PDF is the way most printers prefer to receive book files. Some require the source files (i.e. InDesign) be uploaded with the PDF, but for the most part, they all end up as a high resolution PDF. Any technical questions about uploading should be directed right at the printer.

When the source files are sent to the printer, so are the fonts. There are licenses attached to the fonts and they come through the design program that the designer has.

When a file is uploaded, it goes to a process many call "preflight." That's where they check to see if the files are clean and meeting the printer's standards. Some of the issues they look for are:

- Image resolution
- Bleeds
- Page count
- Page size
- Color format
- Printed in… (on the back cover by the barcode)
- Fonts
- Images
- Highlight/shadow values
- Corrupted files
- Supported file types (images)

If book's text pages are just text without images, then both the digital and offset processing are straight forward. If there are illustrations, photographs, charts, graphs, or color, there is a difference between the two processes. That has to do with the cost of preparing the color plates and the print quality of the grayscale images. That might vary from printer to printer. The quality of the grayscale is far superior with offset. In offset, everything is punchier.

A digital proof is pretty much exactly like the book will look when it's delivered. In the offset proof, the cover is more or less what you'll get with the finished book. The inside is not. It's done on lesser quality paper, not trimmed, and you can see the dots on the pictures, but when you look at the finished version, the pictures are clean. In a color proof, you're not going to see the color exact because the proof paper is different than what was ordered for the book. Paper quality and thickness also changes the color of the finished product.

After the files are checked in preflight, if everything is okay, the proof is generated. This is what the printers print from. Any proof changes are made by the designer, who re-uploads the individual corrected pages. You note the corrections on the form supplied by the printer after marking up the proof, then sign and send everything back to the printer. Every time the printer touches the file, it costs more money. The proof is the last opportunity to look at the book before it rolls off the press.

When the proof goes back to the plant, that's when you can confirm your delivery. Usually the day the finished books leave the plant, they send you an email with the tracking number. The books are generally delivered within the next two business days.

Digital printing, in many cases, takes less time to deliver than offset. It all depends on the schedule at the printer's end. If you can advise the printer of the status of the files, for example, if they are still in layout and you think they might be ready for a certain date, they might be able to save a spot for you in the cue. Keep advising them of the status if there are any delays. Digital books can take five days to four weeks to print. Offset can take two weeks to eight weeks. Sometimes books can stay in preflight for a week to two weeks, depending on the printer's schedule.

Paper stock

You can order any kind of paper you want, but if you can use the in-house stock, it's much more economical. Printers will have samples you can see prior to ordering.

There are coated and uncoated stocks. What might be available one year, may not be available the next year. One of the reasons is that paper mills are forever closing and merging, plus gas prices and deforestation take its toll on the bottom line. It's why printing costs can be the most expensive part of your book.

Binding

When choosing your binding, think about the purpose of the book. If your book is a workbook or a cookbook, coil binding might be better because the reader doesn't have to fight to keep the pages open.

You can get the lay flat perfect binding, where there is a space between the glued pages and the cover. The integrity of the spine more fragile in this format. There are coil bound books where the cover comes over the coil (wire-o), where you can print on the spine.

Price

With regards to putting the price on the book, that is an individual decision. Pricing is subjective. Look what's on the shelves. What are other books going for in your genre? Then ask yourself honestly, what would you pay for the same book if someone else wrote it?

Production

Choose a printer that knows book publishing. Will they insert the barcode if you ask them, provide a digital proof of the text, and a digital Kodak proof or color keys of the cover? If your distributor has packaging restrictions, can the printer accommodate them?

You might be surprised to learn that there are few bonafide book publishers in North America. Bowker has a list of US printers, which includes United Graphics of Mattoon, Illinois which will print as low as 1,000 books (most US book printers consider a small run to be 5,000).

For Canadian printers, the list is smaller and includes Friesens, and Houghton Boston, RR Donnelley for offset; Friesens, BlitzPrint for digital. There are certainly other printers that can do the job and do it well, but unless their presses run 24/7 on books, you pay a lot more for them to reconfigure their press – as much as double.

To get an accurate quote, supply the following information:

- Quantity
- Paper stock for both the cover and text
- Is the text in black ink only?
- Is the cover full-color?
- Are there any bleeds?
- How many pages (laid out in graphic design – not from your Word file)
- Type of binding required
- Page size
- How will photos be included in the book? (included in the text pages or by using a separate signature?)

Cheap production is one of the biggest complaints about Print on Demand firms. Also, it may be cheaper to print in China and to use newsprint instead of 50 or 60 pound text paper stock, but those books look like they won't last through the year, let alone standing up to time, like my 1897 copy of Bram Stoker's Dracula.

E-books

Once your book is completed by a graphic designer, it is already an e-book. As a book is sent to the printer in two files (cover and inside), all the graphic designer has to do is combine the two files and save it into a new PDF – a lower resolution PDF that is emailable. There is no special layout, except you can update the copyright page with a new ISBN for the e-book, plus make a couple other adjustments. (It won't be printed in anywhere.)

Process Checklist

ISBN application (when title known)

Completed (final edited) manuscript to layout

CIP application (if required)

Once page count known in layout, can solicit a printing quote

Proof layout, ensure pictures high resolution (minimum 300 dpi)

Proof revisions

When layout finalized, upload to printer

Fix any file issues in preflight

Proof the proof

Step 9

It's All About Sales

The first step starts with the end product

Picture this. You've just heard the most dynamic speaker. At the conclusion of his talk, you rush to the back of the room to purchase his book. At home, you settle into reinforcing what you learned by opening the book. As you begin to read, you're appalled that this eloquent speaker didn't even appear to take time to edit his book. There is no flow to the text and you discover numerous grammatical and spelling errors.

The quality of your product is reflective of the time and effort you put into it. Most people don't have a lot of time on their plate. If that's the case, hire a competent ghostwriter or editor.

Grammar plus proofing equals professionalism.

Don't write a book for the sake of writing a book. What's your purpose for writing it? Why should the reader care?

Looks are everything. Your book is your marketing tool. It offers you instant credibility. Taking the time and effort to ensure it looks as good as it reads is something you will never regret.

Marketing 101

Treat your book as a business.

Marketing is about planting seeds, not sell, sell, sell.

There is a misconception that a book only needs to get into the bookstore to sell itself. Some of the most high profile writers will tell you that this is simply not true. By the time they figured it out, their books were regulated to the bargain bin or returned to the publisher.

Like it or not, as an author, you must become actively involved in promoting your book if you want it to sell. This is automatic with a self-published book. Perhaps the biggest myth in the book publishing world is that a traditional publisher will automatically sell your book.

Authors are not necessarily adept at sales or can come up with creative ideas on their own for the sole purpose of selling their books. Most believe it's the publisher's job to sell the book. The fact is, even though traditional publishers invest money into printing and advances, few, if any, take a proactive approach to selling books. The best they might do is send out a press release, include the book in their buying catalogue, or do a one-shot advertisement. Depending on the scope of the book, the publisher may even pay for some promotional tours.

Having a book in the bookstores is only one step. Just that fact alone can be used to sell it many other ways. Professional speakers will have books available for their keynote and workshop audiences. Musicians can sell their books alongside t-shirts at each of their concerts. Professional athletes can do book signings at a team's community events, offering a percentage to charity. Actors can have their books available for sale at theatres. Talk show hosts and media can reference their books on their shows. There are numerous creative ways to increase sales outside of the bookstores, where the only expense may be to offer 40 percent to the venue for carrying it.

Know what you want to achieve

The first rule of marketing a book is knowing that nobody cares that you wrote it. They don't care what it's about or why you wrote it. They want to know WHY they should invest the hours it will take to read it. They don't want to be sold. They want to know what's in it for them.

Think about how you react when you walk into a furniture store or used car lot and salespeople are clamoring all over each other to get you as their "up." It's how people feel when you use the "you should buy my book" line to everyone you meet. Some people may buy them to get rid of you, but they probably won't read it.

Instead, build yourself up as an expert, a storyteller, an entertainer.

What are the benefits of reading your book?

What sets you apart from the rest of your competitors?

Who will you approach?

What will you say?

When will you do it?

Where are they located?

How will you approach them?

Who are you?

Why should they listen?

What qualifies you to talk about this subject?

How much will you spend?

You may need to spend some money to market. Here are ideas you might consider:

- Bookmarks
- Flyers
- Direct mail packages
- Websites
- Brochures
- Postcards
- Greeting cards
- Calendars
- Trade shows
- Flea market tables

All these things can help sell your book but you will have to invest something to make it happen. Don't rest your laurels on just one outlet. Get the most value for your money.

Consider: taking a sales course, hiring a guerrilla marketer, learning as much as you can about marketing and sales – tap your creative juices by always looking for opportunities.

Consider the bookstores gravy if you get it in but don't rest your marketing success on it. Search for ideas outside the norm.

Who is your target audience? Why would people read your book? *If someone else wrote the same book, why would you read it?*

You may want to test the waters by polling your family, associates, friends, and strangers.

What else is out there?

Is your idea special?

Is it unique?

If your book is to promote your business, how will it set you ahead of your competitors?

What *service* can you offer in your book that will make people remember you?

What valuable information can you share that will ensure people will keep your book on their shelves for years to come?

Marketing is marketing, regardless of the product. It's thinking creative ideas that get you noticed faster.

- You first look at who your book is targeted to and then go where they go to get them to buy.
- You could start workshops on this topic.
- You are only limited by your imagination.

Be a student of marketing and selling and take ideas from everyone else and maybe adjust them to fit your marketing efforts. (Secrets of Power Marketing by Peter Urs Bender and George Torok is an excellent tool.) Traditional selling and marketing of books is why there were so many books flying off the shelf (I'm joking) when we sit in a bookstore Starbucks for coffee. Traditional efforts are why traditional publishers are going under and amalgamating their business. The marketing doesn't have to be "out there" but there are many fresh ideas around. One afternoon sifting through Google and you'll fill a school notebook. AND it takes some effort. Nothing happens without it. Just like the words of the manuscript, the same process applies: work. There are a gazillion people who will tell you why it won't work. You just need to listen to those who tell you HOW it can work. That separates the girls from the women.

Getting into bookstores

Bookstores will not deal with individual publishers due to numbers. Instead, books must be represented by a middleman: a distributor. One distributor may represent hundreds, even thousands of publishers.

While it is possible for a publisher to actively solicit individual bookstores to carry its books, it is an onerous task and generally only local, independent bookstores will choose to accept them. To reach a larger marketplace, a publisher must *sell* its book to a distributor before it reaches the shelves of a national bookstore chain. The distributor carries the inventory and ships the books to each bookstore as ordered. Returns are sent back to the distributor *at the publisher's expense*. While some percentages vary, bookstores generally take 45 percent of the retail price and the distributor receives 20 percent of the retail price, leaving the balance split between the publisher and author. If the two are separate, the author will receive five and 10 percent. Monies are not usually realized until, at the very minimum, three months after a month's sales.

A good distributor will have a great rapport with the big box chains. In order for a publisher to get its book into a bookstore, the distributor must be convinced that the book will appeal to the general marketplace. In other words, they have to be convinced the book will make money. It's also an exclusive arrangement.

But beware. There are firms masquerading as "distributors," but they are really snakes looking for people to scam. A lot of times these so-called distributors will contact you before you contact them – probably learning about your book from searching the list of new ISBNs. Check them out thoroughly before signing any contract. Also, when Print on Demand firms offer distribution, what they really mean is posting your book on their Website to which the site promotes their interest more than yours.

How long a book remains on the shelves depends on how involved the author becomes in the sales effort. Don't think having it in Borders and Chapters will make you rich.

Book signings

Even if your book is not in a bookstore, you can still promote it through book signings in a bookstore or many other locations. Try

- Libraries
- Eclectic coffee houses
- Retail shops
- Malls
- Flea markets
- Hockey arenas, ball diamonds

If your book is an accounting book, chances are nobody will be interested at the hockey rink or ball diamond, unless there is an accounting association tournament. Make sure your book is a fit; in other words, go where your target audience goes.

Whether you do a signing at a bookstore or another venue, be prepared to answer a lot of questions. Don't sit there and read a newspaper. Look approachable. Smile. Have a pen handy. (Don't rely on the venue to supply one.) Have props to help tweak the interest of passersby. Engage them; bribe them with chocolate.

The author of "Eggs for Shoes," Edie Postill Cole, is a homemaking grandmother with absolutely no fear of approaching anyone who comes within speaking range about her book. She asks everyone, "Would you like to see the book I wrote?" Then she proceeds to tell them what it is about. Her book is in only a handful of local bookstores. She's had very few media interviews but she travels the rural communities and does book signings wherever she can. This woman self-published and has sold over 5,000 copies.

Marketing differently from everybody else

Email marketing

There is a delicate balance here. You MUST avoid spam. Spamming is when you send the same email to everyone at the same time in one shot. How do YOU like getting spam in your own mailbox? If it happens more than once, you usually put that sender on the block sender list or report their ISP. You don't want people to report your ISP for spamming. That means you LOSE your email account.

When it comes to emailing, personalizing is the key. There are many email programs that cost very little, which have attractive design templates and send out mass emails but personalize the message. I use Constant Contact but there are others that are equally as reputable.

If you send the emails out yourself, develop a template where you can personalize EVERY email:

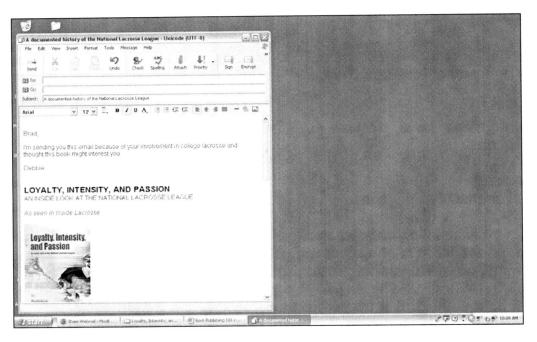

If it's someone you don't know, you can tell them why you think they might be interested. I've sold a few books on this soft sell. You don't blanket send; you send these individually.

Use Google to find the niche market

Fine tune your search as much as possible. You'd be surprised at the number of sites dedicated to certain topics. Look at discussion boards, fan sites, associations – anything that might link the topic of your book. Then you would log onto each of those sites to find a contact and maybe send out the template email – or join the discussion boards. But don't flog your book. Nobody cares. Join a conversation and when you sign off with your name, include: author of…

Niche market associations

These are the places you want to encourage bulk sales. You might consider a discount grid to entice this. Ten percent discount for this many sales; then 15 percent, and 20, etc.

Book launches

Authors can make arrangements to launch a book party at a coffee shop, restaurant, bar, community center, church, and anywhere you can think of where you can invite a large gathering of people and set up a table for signing. Maybe you can strike a deal with the venue and offer them the retailer's discount if they handle the sales and maybe stock your book afterwards. Barrie Reeder, who wrote Confessions of a Small Town Sailor, launched his book party with an open house and invited several neighbors from at least a two-block radius. He presented it as a celebration wine and cheese launch, not putting pressure on guests that they have to buy and sold about 70 books.

Sponsorships

One author sought corporate sponsors to cover the cost of producing his book, which was geared towards adolescents as a history of the area. This might work best when you are well connected and already a good salesman. But, it has to be a win-win. Companies are not going to throw you money just because. You need to have a pretty strong marketing plan to pull this off.

Company newsletters

Many companies produce company newsletters that will not only include internal information, but also an entertaining story or joke to keep the employees engaged. If you contact human resources departments, they just might be looking for story ideas and be open to using excerpts from your book. You would not sell, but in your one- or two-line bio say that you are the author of...to which the excerpt might have came from. There may be online trade and niche sites that are also looking for content and you would handle it the same way.

Amazon

Go to the Amazon Website and look for the Advantage link. There you can set up a vendor account to get your book listed. What you need to know is Amazon takes 55 percent. They will order maybe one or two books at a time and it will cost you nearly the same as your earnings to send the book out. So why do it? It give your book an online presence. If someone heard you wrote a book, their automatic response is to search on Google. If you don't appear, you don't exist. It gives you "free" credibility. It will also reach the readers you might miss otherwise.

A number of organizations sound too good to be true in that they tell you how to become number one on Amazon. Never is it as easy as it sounds, and always they will charge you a handsome fee that will likely be more than you will ever reap in sales. The bottom line, if it sounds too good to be true; it is.

Reviews

The jury is out as to whether using reviews really helps to sell books. Like the snake oil distributors, you'll get several passing themselves off as a reviewer just to get a free book. Never send out a book just because they ask for one. Be discriminate. You will have to comp books as it is – to media, when you're trying to entice bulk sales to associations, and to others that you want to get onboard with a positive impression. Your book is also your own personal brochure. If you are trying to land a contract, leaving the subject with a copy of your book as a thank you for meeting with you may not necessarily get you the contract, but it will get you noticed.

Networking

Networking is the art of making and using contacts. The premise is that people like to do business with people that they know. It is perhaps the best and strongest way to market. However, it is not a quick, overnight result. A couple important things about networking you need to know are a) you never sell on the spot, b) just because a person doesn't appear to be a fit for your book/business, does not mean they don't know someone who is, and c) it's about developing long-term relationships, which means there has to be something in it for the other person.

One of the best approaches to networking is to go into it with the idea of trying to help someone else – perhaps by connecting them with someone they need to know. When you put other people first, they will undoubtedly return the interest. They might suggest people for you to talk to about speaking engagements, retail outlets, or associations. You never know what will grow when you plant the seeds.

A common way to build a network is to join a group. The trick is to pick the right group with the right fit. What you gain from the group will be in direct proportion to what you contribute to the group. Groups can enable you to receive intellectual stimulation from both the peer group and the idea brainstorming sessions.
Groups promote awareness of future trends. You get a sense of having a sounding board away from the office. You trade leads, business cards and shoptalk.

How to network

1. Meet as many people as you can
2. Tell people what you do (low cost advertising)
3. Introduce yourself (act like a host, not a guest)
4. Don't do business while networking (make a date later)
5. Give (do favors) and get (someday you may want one)
6. Follow up
7. Keep in touch
8. Make friends (even if you think you don't need them)
9. Edit your contacts annually (weed the non-productive)

Social networking

This is a new and exciting market that is ever changing and can reach more people than you could ever imagine – for free. Experiment. See what others are doing. Educate yourself on this venue. Popular sites are Facebook, LinkedIn, Twitter, MySpace, Ryze, and there are many more that are directly related to industries. You can start your own social networking site. There is so much out there, you'll never keep up. If you want to know how well social networking can work for you, check out President Barak Obama's election campaign. He still has well over eight million members of his Facebook group. Lady Gaga has over six million.

We are in the middle of a media revolution: traditional is becoming passé. Those that learn and move with the ebb and flow of the Internet will find more success than those stuck in the old traditional formats of how marketing and media was done in the past 50 years.

For example, many have stopped buying newspapers because they are getting their news and information online and through cable television because it's instantaneous; it's easy; and you get a broader viewpoint.

Here are the facts:

- The high fixed costs of printing and distribution are not going down any time soon. Print media is finding itself priced out of the marketplace.
- The Rocky Mountain News closed its doors in February 2009.
- The Philadelphia Inquirer, Baltimore Sun, and Boston Globe shut down their foreign bureaus; Time and Newsweek downsized their foreign correspondents (www.LJWorld.com)
- The Tribune Co., owners of Chicago Tribune and Los Angeles Times, went into bankruptcy proceedings shortly before the Rocky Mountain News went out of business and outsourced its foreign news coverage.
- (Pew Internet and American Life Project November 19 to December 20, 2008): 70 percent Internet users get their news online; 36 percent get their news online daily; 29 percent look for their hobby or interests online daily.
- (Statistics Canada, June 2008): 73 percent of the population 16 and older go online for personal reasons; 68 percent are online every day; men stay online longer than women; most online users earn over $95,000; 84 percent of online users have some post-secondary education
- (The Conference Board and TNS): close to 16 percent of Internet-using US households watch television broadcasts online; 3/5 of those that watch online broadcasts say it's more convenient
- Television networks have lost 17 percent of its 18- to 49-year-old demographic to Internet TV (comScore)
- (Awareness Inc.) 93 percent of organizations surveyed use some form of unpaid social media in an era of declining marketing budgets

YouTube

Like social networking, YouTube is developing its own revolution. More and more authors are creating their own videos and creating even greater exposure. Numerous online radio venues allow you to create your own podcasts.

So when you look at marketing, look at more than just the obvious. Use the Internet to find opportunities. Search for brilliant and creative marketing ideas that are at your fingertips.

However, as you move forward, focus on the message, not the book. Here is an example of marketing innovation from a friend of mine. CoraMarie Clark has branded herself as Toothena the Tooth Fairy. She sent this email to let her friends know about some of the good things that were happening as a result of her efforts.

> Recently, a media company in Calgary filmed a presentation I gave at a school, and then did an interview for a pilot project for a new TV show called Dynamic Philanthropy. The link for the clip is: www.dynamicphilanthropy.com.
>
> The maiden voyage for The Tooth Fairy Children's Foundation is taking place Oct 21 to Nov 14, 2008. As Toothena, I will be giving presentations, visiting, and distributing toothbrushes to children in Kenyan schools and villages. Then, I'll be working with the "Feed the Children" organization (www.feedthechildren.com), the Abandoned Baby Center, and the Maasai Development Project. For the rest of the trip, I will be working with "A Better World Foundation Inc," (www.a-better-world.com), an organization that delivers sustainable foundations necessary to reduce poverty and human suffering.
>
> Once back from Kenya, I'll send you the link for the pictures and report from the trip. Oh, and while there, I'll be attending the opening of a school that's being dedicated to my mom, who taught 42 years. I'm so exciting to see it all come together – thanks to all of you for your love and support!
>
> Let us know if and how you would like to be involved with The Tooth Fairy Children's Foundation.

Website

You definitely need an online presence if you want to get any business in today's world. If you are not online, you do not exist.

Until you can afford to set up your own Website, you can develop your own site through some of the social networking sites or create your own social networking site, such as Morgan Publishing did through www.ning.com. However, this does limit you to accessing only those who are willing to become members of that site.

When you have your own Website, you can set up e-commerce through PayPal. It's a relatively easy and pain-free way to accept credit cards. Getting a merchant account through your bank can be very costly, and unless you are bringing in thousands of dollars a month in credit card payments, it is not worth doing.

Be wary of snakes in this area, too. Do your homework in checking Web designers out. For impressive corporate profiles and sites without e-commerce, www.merlinedge.com does incredible work. For authors and publishers that want to incorporate video, audio, and/or e-commerce, Max Low at www.tigerstorm.com is your man. Also Stuart Crawford will connect you with anything that involves your computer and the Internet: www.stuartcrawford.com.

Step 10

Getting Noticed on a Larger Scale

It's every author's dream. What's the first name that comes to mind to everyone who has ever thought about publishing a book? Oprah.

We all want our books on Oprah but sending her a copy will not get you on her show. Given the reach of her audience, none of us can even begin to imagine how many letters and emails her organization receives in one day. It's why she'll never see most of them. Million dollar empires have legions of staff that handle everything incoming. And if truth be told, much like having a royalty publisher, just because a book or author makes the show, it doesn't mean instant success and truckloads of sales.

Forget Oprah. Concentrate on WHY you have written or are writing your book. Concentrate on your target audience. What does the reader get out of investing their time in turning the pages? It's not about Oprah; it's not about you; it's always about the reader.

So if you concentrate on your book's message, your business, and the notable things you've achieved by being you, if those things stand up and get noticed by your local community, then perhaps spread outward, just maybe, someone like Oprah may notice and call you. And if they don't, it's a pretty good chance you will have impacted someone who really matters.

Media

The media is the message

It's the most overlooked fact by every household, every industry. We don't always like the message the media sends but it's still only a message. Contrary to popular belief, not every reporter or television anchor creates the news to suit their own purpose. The media reflects what people want to hear.

While all forms of media do feature new book releases from time to time, before you run out and call every station to get them to talk about your book, it's important to *understand* the media and the powerful service they provide.

Is it news?

News is, above everything else, important to the reader, listener, or viewer, not you. It has to be interesting and entertaining. And ultimately, it is something other reporters deem important.

This is not news: new products, new service, advertising, YOUR BOOK.

The best way to get the media's attention is find an intriguing angle, human interest, advice, a gimmick, or a really good story. It is what people want to see, hear, and read. You can piggyback onto another story. Has there been a better time to be a financial expert than 2010, except maybe 1930?

If your book is a sales or marketing book, your angle may be helping others reach their potential. If your company is an accounting firm, you can offer tips on how to "beat the tax man." These are angles the general public will find interesting. You have to *sell* the idea to the media with a compelling argument that will convince them you will be an interesting interview or guest. And having a clip of you speaking on YouTube might not hurt.

Other ways to solicit the media to get interested in your book:

- Respond to an industry trend
- Use statistics to tie into a survey
- Local angle
- Comment on an industry study
- Public service: offering of tips, taking a leadership role in your industry

When the media does call

- Be available
- Be prepared
- Keep it simple, don't ramble on and for goodness sake, don't go "my book this, my book that"
- Don't lie and don't be confrontational

Working the media

First, understand the terminology of the three invitations used when soliciting the media.

Press Release	Public Service Announcement	Media Advisory
"Sell" the media on penning an article	Educate the public, raise awareness, recruit volunteers	Invitation to the media to attend event or press conference
Can't appear as advertising	Non-profit, public interest	When
Most will hit the garbage or "File 13"	Media partnership, looking for free space (advertising) rather than an article	Where – is there good visual for videographers? Is there parking?
Stands alone; enough information to write a short article	Brief and to the point	What – identify the newsworthiness of the event, give some hints
Inverted pyramid structure	Maximum one page	Maximum one page
Maximum 1 ½ pages		

Sending out a press release is like sending out a pitch to a publisher. In the large centers, each reporter receives at least 150 press releases a day. How will yours get noticed? Start with the subject line (if emailing). Like mainstream book publishers, mainstream media will not open attachments. Any communication must be in the content of the email.

Backgrounders

These are included with your press kits and give reporters a bit more information so they don't have to look too far when writing the story. Backgrounders might include

- Fact sheets
- Case studies
- Biographies
- Contact or resource sheets
- Important press articles, etc that support position
- Pertinent newsletters
- Media guides
- Legislative updates
- Policy descriptions
- General information on organization
- History
- Facts addressing and why important (use statistics)
- Services to community
- People who benefit from services (think on broad terms)
- Function: mission statement
- Role in service area - where company fits in marketplace and community
- Performance indicators
- How does company compare to competitors

Writing a press release

Organizing the content:

- Include all facts reporter needs to file story
- Inverted pyramid structure: starting with a conclusion, then supporting facts and the least interesting
- Attention-grabbing lead that summarizes the story
- ### or -30- signals end of document
- If more than one page, write continued at bottom of first page
- Second page: one-word "slug" indicating page 2 i.e. Book Publishing 101/page 2
- Use letterhead, date, contact information
- Make it short and sweet

There is such a thing as a no news press release. You might provide a response to external news, or an industry trend. You can use statistics to tie a survey to the message. Use a local angle. Comment on an industry study.

Here's how a press release might be formulated.

Let's say we are the marketing firm for former Canadian Prime Minister Jean Chretien as he is about to leave office to start a new business. Here are some notes about the man that we might have gleaned from interviews and our research about him. This is what we know:

- He is one of the western world's top leaders
- He oversees millions
- He has the ability to solicit major funding for undefined ventures
- He is unafraid to take risks
- He has the courage to stand by principles, regardless of how popular
- He is concerned about the welfare of others and encourages diversity by providing homes for immigrants shunned by other countries
- He is a trendsetter, capable of setting benchmarks for others to aspire to (Kyoto)
- He is creative (accounting)

The following is the press release for his new venture:

For Immediate Release
January 22, 2003

New Career for Prime Minister

It's official. Prime Minister Jean Chretien is leaving politics. He is about to embark on a new journey into the world of fashion design. Throughout his political career, it's been one of Chretien's secret passions.

"The sewing machine has always helped me relieve the stress of having the weight of a country on my shoulders," admits Chretien. *"The passion goes back to my law studies at Laval University. After my meetings with the Liberal Club, I would come home and sew. Each stitch would represent a solution to a problem."*

Chretien, 68, who has spent over nine years at the helm of one of the world's leading countries, will start his new venture as early as March 2003. Designs By J.C. will cater to professionals and people on the move. The Right Honorable Sheila Copps has modeled the Prime Minister's designs for years. Expect to see his creations to reach the retail market this fall.

Prime Minister Jean Chretien has dedicated his life to politics and the Federal Liberal Party. His wife, Aline, supports his new venture. His three children, France, Hubert, and Michel, will help market the designs.

For more information contact:

Right Honorable Sheila Copps
House of Commons
Ottawa, Ontario
(604) 555 – 1212
www.designsbyjc.ca

Press Kits

These would include:

- News release one or two pages; include a media advisory only if you don't include a press release as a reminder to reporter as to what event was about
- Background material supporting news, credentialing organization
- Information should be clear, concise, well-documented and credible; focus on key elements; too much information can take away from focus
- Speaker biographies
- Background statement includes name of organization, contact info, purpose, recent work

Media events

Conducting a media event will depend on whether or not the event is newsworthy. Timing is everything and you will need financial and human resources to put it together.

Examples of media events

- Breakfasts and luncheons – best for national and international stories on non-breaking news
- Briefings and press conferences – for breaking news and inform on issue
- Conference calls for breaking news – targets reporters that are not available locally
- Editorial board meeting – one-on-one with editors, editorial boards and other writers; best at beginning of a media campaign; best to approach when not in a defensive position – to provide information; present a viewpoint or raise general awareness about your issues only; not to berate media; develops relationship
- Breakfasts – helps develop relationships, good for questions and answers
- Gimmicks and non-news items – draws attention to something you've had trouble getting the media interested in; best targets are soft news sections (fashion, food, homes)

Planning a press event

Use a checklist for: furniture, equipment, facilities, other logistics

- Notify media
- RSVP list
- Credentials
- Registration table, if necessary
- Refreshments
- Timing
- Speakers/spokesperson

- Materials: media kit, press release no longer than 1 ½ pages; trinkets will not convince reporters of its worthiness
- Audio visual, microphones; test equipment prior to everyone's arrival
- Allow for pool feeds, where reporters can plug into to record speakers during event
- Allow space for one-on-one or scrum interviews following news conference
- Follow-up

Basic tips

- If using PowerPoint, limit to five slides
- Know what the reporter has published before making first contact
- Get the facts quickly to the right people, particularly if they have asked for them
- Put full corporate contact and product summary information in all releases and Web material
- Don't send unsolicited email attachments
- Avoid sending out a group email with entire press list in header
- Fix factual inaccuracies immediately
- Have someone on hand to explain what others may not understand
- If you don't know the answer, find out and get back to them promptly
- Understand the power and limitations of freelance reviewers
- Be specific in your message; what makes this newsworthy to writers who receive 25 other press releases in the same day? Make it easy on the reporter.

Talking to the media

- Be available
- Be prepared
- Know your subject
- Know what the reporters want
- KISS: keep it simple; don't belabour the point
- Never lie; if you don't know the answer, say so and try and find out
- Stay on top of current events, particularly as it pertains to your industry
- Anticipate some of the questions and what your answer will be; be proactive on negative stuff
- Be presentable; look professional, smile
- Pay attention to how reporters interpret what you say and correct if necessary but do it tactfully and politely; never ridicule; put onus on your delivery rather than reporter's listening skills
- Clarify or elaborate when needed

Step 11

Other Things You Need to Know

Drive your computer safely online

Anti-virus and other protective software are as important to your computer as its operating system. Without it, you're driving blindfolded, backwards on the highway at 100 miles per hour. It's not a matter of if you'll crash, it's when.

There are many gremlins, hackers, and cyber-mosquitoes trying to land inside your computer every second of every minute. Don't believe me? Check the activity logs on your anti-virus software. For example, looking at one day's log:

8:57:23 PM, unauthorized access logged and stopped – 17 times

8:57:22 PM, unauthorized access logged and stopped – 13 times

10:29:49 – intrusion prevention monitoring 578 signatures

10:29:48 – intrusion prevention monitoring 578 signatures

In fact, if you don't have anti-virus software, I suggest you shut down this very minute and run, don't walk, to Wal-Mart, Staples, or wherever the CDs are sold. I like the CD because if you ever need to reload it (re computer system upgrades, etc.), it's much easier and cheaper than trying to buy another download off the Website. Some anti-virus software companies will allow you unlimited downloads. Consider it computer insurance and the cost of driving your computer online. Without it, you should be arrested for driving without insurance and putting everyone in your address book at risk of a fatal virus or worm. This software updates daily for a year. I recommend retrieving updates every day.

The other two items you need are a firewall and a spyware zapper. You'd be amazed at the alerts on these logs, too. You can just be comforted to know it's working without having to see it working.

There are spyware zappers you can buy, but one of the best, and highly recommended by Microsoft, is Ad-Aware. The good part is you can download this for free from Lavasoft. It zaps much of the spyware that comes with pretty much every spam email plus those excruciating elongated text forwarded jokes and e-cards. Spyware is evil because it launches stuff inside your computer so people can see what you're doing, and some might find a way to infiltrate your files. If enough spyware accumulates, it can significantly slow down your computer.

The Internet is great for opening a lot of doors re opportunity (work-wise), research, etc, but there are a lot of trolls hiding under the bridge waiting to pounce. I look at buying protective software every year like car insurance. You have to or you risk paying through the nose when a virus crashes your computer. A firewall doesn't really stop a lot from getting in, but it helps keep hackers at bay. (Why would anyone want to hack your computer? Two words: identity theft.)

Anti-virus software is your number one priority. If you only use one of the three, that should be your first choice. Your second priority would be a firewall, and third: Ad Aware. These three things make that big scary world of cyberspace a lot easier to maneuver and you can go about your business virtually undetected.

Back up, back up, back up!

It amazes me how many people do not back up their work. You invest how many hours in producing your manuscript? And it can all disappear in the flick of a power surge. When it does, you can never rewrite every word you wrote, probably not even a paragraph.

You might back up your work on a CD once the project is complete. If you do, keep one copy onsite for easy reference and another offsite. So if your house burns down with everything in it, you will still have your files.

While your work is in progress, use the SAVE button as if it were the space bar. Trust me on this. I was writing an article for the Calgary Herald and after penning the third paragraph, a power surge zapped my Word file and I couldn't recover what I had written. I had to rewrite. Fortunately it was only three paragraphs, but it was a chore to try and rebuild them. I have used the SAVE button twice in this paragraph alone.

When I'm ready to shut down at the day's end, or sometimes when I take a break, I will email the latest version of the manuscript to myself on my Hotmail account (which I use as a backup) before I get a chance to save the work on a portable backup device (USB key). Again, if something happens, you can still access your emails offsite.

Before you give up:

When everything seems overwhelming, when you think you have no business writing a book, when you choose to listen to everyone telling you that you cannot do it, here are some warm fuzzies to keep you going.

- The 27th publisher accepted Richard Bach's "Jonathan Livingston Seagull"

- "Moby Dick's" Herman Melville almost gave up because he was discouraged from failure

- Hans Christian Anderson was told his stories were unsuitable for children

- Margaret Mitchell's "Gone With the Wind" was turned down at least 25 times

- Rudyard Kipling was fired from his job as a reporter at a San Francisco daily because he "couldn't use the English language"

Canonero II

When you ask someone who their childhood sports hero was, you'll likely hear answers like Michael Jordan, Wayne Gretzky, Cassius Clay, Magic Johnson, or Pele. But when you read the following paragraphs, you'll understand why it was a horse that inspired me. It was a horse that showed me I could be anything I wanted to be. It was a horse that taught me perseverance, to forge ahead against all odds, and to tune out the negative voices. This horse was not just any ordinary horse. He was Canonero II.

Sometimes stories are so good; they just have to be true.

Canonero II was bred by Edward B. Benjamin in Kentucky, in 1969. Being born with a crooked right foreleg deemed that this young bay colt would have no future in thoroughbred racing. He was actually said to be named after Latin American street musicians. Given away, he was put up for auction shortly afterwards.

Edgar Caibett had no idea what the future might hold when he purchased this sad little yearling for $1,200 at the 1969 Keeneland September yearling sale (a fall sale for racehorses with a pedigree and/or conformation not up to the required standards of most summer-sale yearlings). But he shipped the colt to his native Venezuela, and then gave the colt away as a wedding gift to his son-in-law.

As a two year old, Canonero II started to earn an undistinguished record in racing and traveled all over the western hemisphere to participate in numerous cheaper races. It was joked that he had logged enough air time to qualify as a pilot.

Sent to the United States, in 1971, to be trained by unorthodox methods by a little known trainer (Juan Arias), Canonero II was entered into the Triple Crown.

At first, the Kentucky Derby representative thought it was a joke to see this name on the ballot. The horse was so lightly regarded in the race that he was regulated to the mutual field. For betting purposes, it's a single grouping that the track handicapper uses as a catchall for several horses thought to have little chance of winning.

Canonero II's only escorts to the Derby from Venezuela were the teenage son of his owner Pedro Baptista and crates of ducks and chickens. His first flight was missed due to a fire in the plane's engine, and the second flight had mechanical problems. Upon his arrival in Miami, it was discovered they forgot his customs papers. He spent four days in quarantine. After his release, the van he was transported in broke down. The entire episode of travel caused the horse to lose 80 pounds.

From the 18th spot in a 20-horse field, the young colt took the world by surprise and won the race by 3 ¾ length in what was the biggest upset in horse racing history.

When TV commentators tried to interview trainer Juan Arias and jockey Gustavo Avila after the Kentucky Derby, they quickly learned they would need a translator. However, one was never sought as Canonero II wasn't considered high enough to warrant the effort.

Canonero II, the unlikely hero of the Kentucky Derby, set a new track record for time in winning the Preakness Stakes.

Now taken seriously and drawing a cult following, particularly from the Latino community, Canonero II was stricken with a foot infection several days before the Belmont Stakes. He did manage to take the lead but clearly struggled and finished fourth, narrowly missing a win of the anticipated Triple Crown. He still managed to win the Eclipse Award for three-year-old colts.

Canonero II was sold to Hall of Fame trainer Buddy Hirsch. He raced his best race of his career in the Stymie Handicap at Belmont Park in 1972, defeating champion Riva Ridge.

Near the end of 1972, Canonero II was retired to stud. He died nine years later in 1981.

Would you believe there has not been a book written about Canonero II? You'll even be hard-pressed to find an article, other than mine. All the more reason to use this horse as an example for what we can achieve, even if we fall under the radar.

With all the information you've learned here, you have everything in you that is capable of producing a well developed manuscript and to take it to that next level: a book in print. So what are you waiting for? Go write something.

Resources

These are just a handful of resources you can access for more information about publishing, writing, editing, and project management. To find more sources, go to www.google.ca or www.google.com and key in what you're looking for.

Trademark/Entertainment Lawyer:

Wayne Logan: www.fieldlaw.com, wlogan@fieldlaw.com
www.inventsai.com

Copyright Information:

US Copyright Office: www.copyright.gov
Access Copyright, The Canadian Copyright Licensing Agency, www.accesscopyright.ca

Library of Congress:

www.loc.gov

National Library of Canada - Cataloguing in Publication:

http://www.collectionscanada.gc.ca/index-e.html

American ISBN:

www.bowker.com

Canadian ISBN:

http://www.collectionscanada.gc.ca/isn/041011-1030-e.html

American Publishers:

http://www.publishers.org
www.booklocker.com

Canadian Publishers:

http://www.publishers.ca

American Authors Association:

http://www.americanauthorsassociation.com

Canadian Authors Association:

http://www.canauthors.org/links/writing.html

Online Bookstores:

www.amazon.com
www.borders.com
www.barnes&noble.com
www.chapters.indigo.com

Writing:

www.writersweekly.com
http://www.writersonlineworkshops.com/
www.writtenword.org

Editing:

http://www.copydesk.org
http://www.press.uchicago.edu/Misc/Chicago
www.editors.ca

Book Printers:

United Graphics www.unitedgraphicsinc.com
Friesens Book Division www.friesens.com
Houghton Boston www.houghtonboston.com
BlitzPrint www.blitzprint.com
RR Donnelley www.rrdonnelley.com

Marketing and Promotion:

Coauthors of Secrets of Power Marketing (Stoddart, 1999): www.torok.com
www.pma-online.org/index
www.marketingpower.com
www.bookmarketingworks.com
www.rickfrishman.com (check out his Author 101 series)
www.parapublishing.com

Social Networking:

www.facebook.com
www.linkedin.com
www.twitter.com
www.myspace.com

www.ryze.com
http://morganjamespublishing.ning.com
www.squidoo.com
www.yahoo.com
www.ziggs.com

Blog Hosts:

www.bloggernews.net
www.ezinearticles.com
www.myarticlearchive.com
www.wordpress.com
www.xanga.com
www.blogger.com

Electronic Hosts:

www.youtube.com
www.mypodcast.com
www.podcast.com

Press Releases:

www.newsbureau.ca
www.prwebdirect.com
www.pr.prlog.org
www.wireservice.ca
www.marketwire.com

About the Author

People from all over North America have been coming to Debbie Elicksen to ask about book publishing. As a book publishing expert, she works hand in hand with authors and companies that produce books, to which many use to market their businesses.

Creating and editing words has played a large role in her primary work. She has authored and published nine books, including the bestselling *Self-Publishing 101* (Self-Counsel Press). She has edited, ghosted, and project managed at least 100 books for others, is a member of the Independent Publishers Association of Canada and Canadian Association of Professional Speakers.

Elicksen is a sports writer and has been covering the National Hockey League for over 16 years. She has had a weekly NHL column on www.nbcsports.com and has written and reported for several other publications and sports services, such as the The Fischler Report, ESPN/PA and Philadelphia Sportsticker, the New England Sports Journal, and www.maxhockey.com. Her sports books include: "Inside the NHL Dream" (behind the scenes look at the NHL), "Positive Sports," "Creating a Legacy," "Future Prospects" (behind the scenes of major junior hockey), and "Loyalty, Intensity, and Passion" (behind the scenes of the National Lacrosse League). She also works with Hockey Canada on its alumni newsletter.

With several years experience working in both amateur and professional sports administration in hockey, baseball, and football, she was a volunteer with the Hockey Media Committee for the 1988 Olympic Winter Games, played a key role in junior football in Canada for 18 years, and was the first woman to headman a football conference in Canada as president of the Prairie Football Conference. She sat on the City of Calgary Sport Policy Steering Committee. As public relations director for the Edmonton Trappers Baseball Club, she worked closely with the California Angels and was responsible for overseeing game day operations, media liaison, staff, and community events.

Book Publishing 101 Audio
ISBN 978-0-9865956-1-5
http://www.freelancepublishing.net/publishing_products.htm

10 Steps to Book Publishing

1. What to write?

2. Your book's resume

3. Treat your book like a new business

4. Sculpting your masterpiece

5. Dispelling the myths of traditional publishing

6. When to publish the book yourself

www.bookpublishing101.net

7. The first step in producing a professional product: getting your book to layout

8. The final product

9. It's all about sales

10. Getting noticed on a larger scale

Self-Publishing 101
ISBN 978-1-55180-639-6
Self-Counsel Press
Available at most North American bookstores and Amazon

Connect with the author -

www.bookpublishing101.net

http://debbieelicksen.blogspot.com/

www.twitter.com/bookpublish101

www.twitter.com/gridironchick

www.linkedin.com/in/freelancecommunications

www.facebook.com/debbie.elicksen

www.youtube.com/bookpublishing101

www.youtube.com/delicksen

Canadian Association of Professional Speakers:
http://bureau.espeakers.com/caps/speaker.php?sid=15005&showreturntoresults=true

http://www.speakersite.com/profile/DebbieElicksen

http://www.scribd.com/FreelancePublishing

LaVergne, TN USA
15 October 2010
200851LV00001B/1/P